The Magic Wand and Other Bright Experiments on Light and Color

THE EXPLORATORIUM SCIENCE SNACKBOOK SERIES

*The Cheshire Cat and Other Eye-Popping
Experiments on How We See the World*

*The Magic Wand and Other Bright
Experiments on Light and Color*

And coming in spring of 1996 . . .

*The Cool Hot Rod and Other Electrifying
Experiments on Energy and Matter*

*The Spinning Blackboard and Other Dynamic
Experiments on Force and Motion*

The Magic Wand and Other Bright Experiments on Light and Color

THE EXPLORATORIUM SCIENCE SNACKBOOK SERIES

PAUL DOHERTY, DON RATHJEN
and the Exploratorium Teacher Institute

JOHN WILEY & SONS, INC.
New York · Chichester · Brisbane · Toronto · Singapore

Development and Testing   Teachers of the Exploratorium Teacher Institute
Photography   Esther Kutnick, Susan Schwartzenberg, Amy Snyder
Illustrations   Larry Antila, Jad King, Arthur Koch, Luisa Kolla, Peter Olguin

This text is printed on acid-free paper.

The publisher and the authors have made every reasonable effort to insure that the experiments and activities in the book are safe when conducted as instructed but assume no responsibility for any damage caused or sustained while performing the experiments or activities in this book. Parents, guardians, and/or teachers should supervise young readers who undertake the experiments and activities in this book.

Library of Congress Cataloging-in-Publication Data:

Doherty, Paul.
    The magic wand and other bright experiments on light and color /
  Paul Doherty, Don Rathjen, and the Exploratorium Teacher Institute.
        p.   cm. — (The Exploratorium science snackbook series)
      Includes index.
      ISBN 0-471-11515-0 (pbk.)
    1. Light—Experiments—Juvenile literature.   2. Color—Experiments—Juvenile literature. [1. Light—Experiments.   2. Color—Experiments.   3. Experiments.]
  I. Rathjen, Don.   II. Exploratorium Teacher Institute (San Francisco, Calif.)
  III. Title.   IV. Series.
  QC360.D64   1995
  535'.078—dc20   94-47035

Printed in the United States of America

10 9 8 7 6 5 4 3 2 1

To the many teachers of the Exploratorium Teacher Institute

who enthusiastically developed and tested

the materials in this book.

Contents

Welcome to the Exploratorium Science Snackbook Series

This book is full of Snacks . . .

. . . but they're not the kind you eat. They're the kind you can learn from and have fun with.

Exploratorium Science Snacks are miniature versions of some of the most popular exhibits at the Exploratorium, San Francisco's famed museum of science, art, and human perception.

What's different about the Exploratorium?

For lack of a better description, the Exploratorium calls itself a "museum." But the half-million visitors who come through the doors each year don't find hushed corridors, watchful guards, or "do not touch" signs. Instead, they walk into a cavernous space filled with whirring, buzzing, spinning things, where people of all ages are smiling and laughing and calling to each other to "Come see this!" and "Hey, look at that!"

At the Exploratorium, you can touch a tornado, look inside your eye, or leave your shadow on a wall. You can pull a giant bubble over your head, sing your way through a maze, or tour a pitch-dark labyrinth using only your sense of touch. When you're done, you might find that you understand a little more about weather, or your senses, or the nature of a bubble film, than you've ever understood before.

So what's a Science Snack?

Since the museum opened in 1969, teachers from the San Francisco Bay Area have brought their classes on field trips to the Exploratorium. When we began putting this book together, we decided to do just the opposite: We wanted to take the exhibits to the kids.

For three years, nearly one hundred teachers worked with staff members to create scaled-down versions of Exploratorium exhibits. The results were dozens of exciting "Snacks"— miniature science exhibits that teachers could make using common, inexpensive, easily available materials. By using Snacks in their classrooms, teachers can climb out of their textbooks and join their students in discovering science for themselves.

What's in a Snack?

The Snacks in this book are divided into easy-to-follow sections that include instructions, advice, and helpful hints.

Each Snack begins with a drawing of the original, full-sized exhibit on the museum floor and a photograph of the scaled-down version that you can make yourself. A short paragraph introduces the exhibit. There's a list of the materials needed and suggestions on how to find them. Other sections give assembly instructions, contain descriptions of how to use the completed exhibits, and explain the science behind them. Most of the Snacks can be completed by one person. If a partner or adult help is needed, this is indicated. A section called "etc." offers interesting bits of additional scientific and historic information.

What can you do with a Snack?

The original collection of 107 Science Snacks was published in a single volume called *The Exploratorium Science Snackbook.* Although the book was written for local high school science teachers, it wasn't long before we began to realize that Snacks were really getting around. Within a week of publication, for instance, we received a message from a teacher in the Australian outback who needed help finding materials.

We heard from elementary school teachers and university professors. Art teachers were using Snacks, as were shop teachers and math teachers. Sixth-graders at one school were building their own miniature science museum. At another school, an ESL (English as a Second Language) teacher found that building Snacks helped her students interact more: Those who understood science best were helping those more adept at building things, and all were getting better at communicating with each other.

And it wasn't just teachers who found Snacks useful: Children were bringing Snacks home to their families. Scouts were using Snacks to help get science badges; Snacks were making appearances at science fairs, birthday parties, and impromptu "magic" shows.

Try it for yourself!

Until now, Science Snacks were available only to teachers. The books in this series now make Science Snacks available to anyone interested in learning about science, or helping others learn about science. Try it for yourself! You might be delighted to find how well hands-on discovery works.

Acknowledgments

The production of the original *Exploratorium Science Snackbook*, upon which this book is based, was made possible by a grant from

The Telesis Foundation

The Snackbook was developed by the Teacher Institute, a part of the Exploratorium Regional Science Resource Center, which is funded in part by

California Department of Education
National Science Foundation
Walter S. Johnson Foundation

What This Book Is About

Take a look out your window on a sunny day. What do you see?

Whatever the scenery outside your window, one answer is always true: You see light. It's really the only thing you can see, the only thing that your eyes can detect. You see trees or cars or clouds because sunlight is bouncing off these things and getting into your eyes. All the colors you see come from light. The grass looks green because it reflects the green of sunlight and absorbs the other colors. A brilliant rainbow shines in the spray of a sunlit fountain because droplets of water spread white light out to reveal its hidden colors. A soap bubble shimmers with iridescence because white light reflected by the two sides of the thin soap film combines in a way that removes some colors and reveals others. Your eyes are designed to detect that light and analyze the information it carries, making an image of the world so that you can see the view—or read this sentence.

The sunlight that reveals the world outside your window begins with the vibration of electrons, the negatively charged particles that orbit the nucleus of an atom. Vibrating electrons in the atmosphere of the sun send light out in all directions. When sunlight gets in your eyes, light that has crossed 93 million miles makes electrons at the back of your eye wiggle, echoing the original vibration of electrons on the sun eight minutes before. Wiggling electrons in your eye create the image of the world that you see.

That's one way to describe light—you can say where it begins and what it does. It's much more difficult to describe what light actually is. For centuries, scientists have been experimenting with light and trying to come up with a description that would explain the observations that they made. Along the way, they came up with two alternatives. You can think of light as a wave, like the waves in the ocean. That description will help explain some of the things that light does—such as the way a beam of light bends when it moves from air into water. Or you can think of light as a stream of particles (called photons), and that will help explain other aspects of light's behavior—like the way certain materials glow under ultraviolet light. But neither description alone can completely explain all the things light does.

However you describe it, light is fascinating stuff to experiment with. The instructions in this book will help you make your own observations about light and how it behaves. Though light is mysterious and tricky, these experiments require basic materials, such as mirrors and magnifying lenses and fish tanks and water.

What can you do with such simple equipment? You can bend light, for one thing. That's called refraction, and lenses do it. You can bounce light around with mirrors and build an exhibit that lets you peer into infinity, or one that puts you inside a kaleidoscope, or one that creates an image that looks so real that you want to reach out and touch it.

You can investigate what happens when light waves meet and mix—in the thin film of a soap bubble or the gap between two plates of glass. Or you can sort light waves, so that you have a set that are all wiggling in the same direction. That's called polarization. Polarized sunglasses eliminate glare and work by blocking all the light waves that wiggle in a particular direction.

Taken together, these experiments let you get a handle on something that you can't even touch—that mysterious stuff we call light. Have fun!

Blue Sky

Now you can explain why the sky is blue and the sunset is red.

▶ When sunlight travels through the atmosphere, blue light scatters more than the other colors, leaving a dominant yellow-orange hue to the transmitted light. The scattered light makes the sky blue; the transmitted light makes the sunset reddish orange.

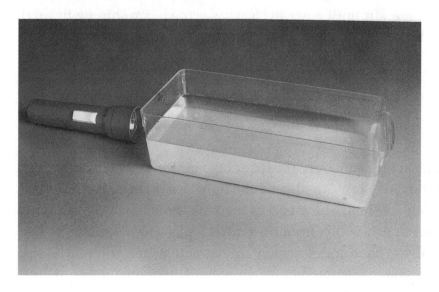

Materials ▶ A transparent plastic box, or a large beaker, jar, or aquarium.

▶ A flashlight or projector (either a slide or filmstrip projector).

▶ Powdered milk.

▶ Polarizing filter (such as the lens from an old pair of polarized sunglasses).

▶ Blank white card for image screen.

▶ Paper hole-punch.

▶ Optional: Unexposed (black) 35 mm slide or photographic film, or an index card cut to slide size.

Assembly
(15 minutes or less)

Fill the container with water. Place the light source so that the beam shines through the container. Add powdered milk a pinch at a time; stir until you can clearly see the beam shining through the liquid.

To Do and Notice
(15 minutes or more)

Look at the beam from the side of the tank and then from the end of the tank. You can also let the light project onto a white card, which you hold at the end of the tank. From the side, the beam looks bluish-white; from the end, it looks yellow-orange.

If you have added enough milk to the water, you will be able

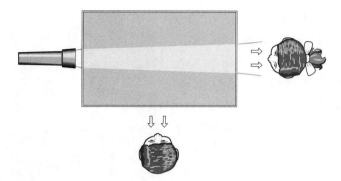

to see the color of the beam change from blue-white to yellow-orange along the length of the beam.

If you want to look at a narrower beam of light, use a paper hole-punch to punch a hole in the unexposed black slide or in a piece of 35 mm film, or even in an index card cut to size. Place the slide, film, or index card in the projector. (Do not hold it in front of the lens.) Focus the projector to obtain a sharp beam.

What's Going On?

The sun produces white light, which is made up of light of all colors: red, orange, yellow, green, blue, indigo, violet. Light is a wave, and each of these colors corresponds to a different frequency, and therefore wavelength, of light. The colors in the rainbow spectrum are arranged according to their frequency: violet, indigo, and blue light have a higher frequency than red, orange, and yellow light.

When the white light from the sun shines through the earth's atmosphere, it collides with gas molecules. These molecules scatter the light.

The shorter the wavelength of light, the more it is scattered by the atmosphere. Because it has a shorter wavelength, blue light is scattered ten times more than red light.

Blue light also has a frequency that is closer to the resonant

frequency of atoms than that of red light. That is, if the electrons bound to air molecules are pushed, they will oscillate with a natural frequency that is even higher than the frequency of blue light. Blue light pushes on the electrons with a frequency that is closer to their natural resonant frequency than that of red light. This causes the blue light to be reradiated out in all directions, in a process called *scattering.* The red light that is not scattered continues on in its original direction. When you look up in the sky, the scattered blue light is the light that you see.

Why does the setting sun look reddish orange? When the sun is on the horizon, its light takes a longer path through the atmosphere to your eyes than when the sun is directly overhead. By the time the light of the setting sun reaches your eyes, most of the blue light has been scattered out. The light you finally see is reddish orange, the color of white light minus blue.

Violet light has an even shorter wavelength than blue light: It scatters even more than blue light does. So why isn't the sky violet? Because there is just not enough of it. The sun puts out much more blue light than violet light, so most of the scattered light in the sky is blue.

○ ○ ○ ○ ○ ○   **etc.**   ○ ○ ○ ○ ○ ○

Scattering can polarize light. Place a polarizing filter between the projector and the tank. Turn the filter while one person views the transmitted beam from the top and another views it from the side. Notice that when the top person sees a bright beam, the side person will see a dim beam, and vice versa.

You can also hold the polarizing filter between your eyes and the tank and rotate the filter to make the beam look bright or dim. The filter and the scattering polarize the light. When the two polarizations are aligned, the beam will be bright; when they are at right angles, the beam will be dim.

Scattering polarizes light because light is a transverse wave. The direction of the transverse oscillation of the electric field is called the *direction of polarization of light.*

The beam of light from the slide projector contains photons of light that are polarized in all directions: horizontally, vertically, and all angles in between. Consider only the vertically polarized light passing through the tank. This light can scatter to the side and remain vertically polarized, but it cannot scatter upward! To retain the characteristic of a transverse wave after scattering, only the vertically polarized light can be scattered sideways, and only the horizontally polarized light can be scattered upward. This is shown in the drawing below.

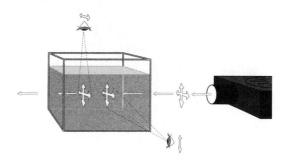

Bone Stress

Polarized light reveals stress patterns in clear plastic.

▶ When certain plastics are placed between two pieces of polarizing material, their stress patterns become dramatically visible in a brightly colored display. A stressed plastic object can be used to illustrate stresses found in bones.

Materials ▸ Overhead projector and screen.

▸ 2 polarizing filters. (If polarizing material is not readily available, you can use two lenses from an old pair of polarizing sunglasses.)

▸ A transparent plastic picnic fork, or thin pieces (about ¹⁄₁₆ to ⅛ inch [.16 to .33 cm]) of transparent plastic. (Plastic from cassette tape cases works well.)

Assembly
(15 minutes or less)

Set up your overhead projector so that the light shines on the screen.

Place one of the filters on the stage of the overhead projector. If the second piece of polarizer is large enough to cover most of the lens on the arm of the projector, then tape it there. (See drawing.)

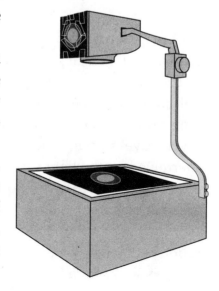

If you are using the lens from a pair of sunglasses, then devise a stand to hold the lens a few inches above the stage of the projector, right over the first filter.

If you are using thin plastic, such as the plastic from a cassette tape case, cut it into the shape of letters that can be flexed (C, J, S, K, etc., or any other shape that can be flexed).

To Do and Notice
(5 minutes or more)

Hold the fork or plastic letter above the first filter and below the second filter. Induce stress by squeezing the tines of the fork together or deforming the letter. Notice the colored stress pattern in the image of the plastic that is projected on the screen. Try rotating one of the polarizing filters. Some orientations will give more dramatic color effects than others.

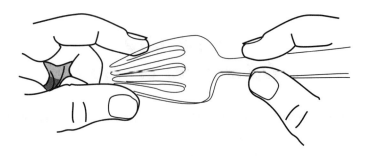

What's Going On?

The first polarizing filter limits the vibration of light waves to one plane—that is, it *polarizes* the light.

The white light of the overhead projector is made up of light of all colors. The plastic breaks the light waves that make up each color into two perpendicularly polarized waves. These two waves travel through the plastic at different speeds, which are determined by the light's color. When the two waves meet and recombine, they produce a polarization unique to that color. The direction of polarization determines whether light of a certain color can pass through the second polarizing filter. If the new direction of polarization lines up with the second filter, light of that color passes through the filter and you see it. If the new direction of polarization does not line up with the second filter, light of that color is blocked. By rotating the filter, you can let different colors pass through, and the colors you observe will change.

Stressing the plastic alters its structure, which affects how rapidly light of different polarizations travels through the plastic. Where colored patterns change rapidly, stress is high. Where colored regions are spread out and change gradually, stress is low. Sharp corners, or areas that have been cut or stamped, are usually areas of stress concentration. Changing the stresses in the plastic will change the color pattern in the plastic.

Stress patterns and concentrations like the ones visible in the plastic are also present in your bones, as they flex under the daily loads imposed upon them.

The college editions of *Conceptual Physics* by Paul Hewitt (HarperCollins College Publishers, New York, 1993) contain an excellent diagram and explanation of the formation of colors by polarized light traveling through plastic or similar material. You will need to have a basic understanding of vectors to read this material. For related information, see the *Polarized-Light Mosaic* Snack.

Bridge Light

Use a thin layer of air trapped between two pieces of Plexiglas™ to produce rainbow-colored interference patterns.

▶ *When light hits two slightly separated transparent surfaces, part of the light will be reflected from each surface. If the distance between the surfaces is a multiple of half or whole wavelengths of the light, constructive and destructive interference will occur, producing an* **interference pattern.**

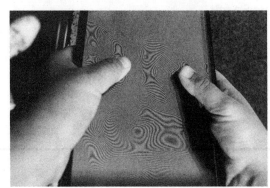

Materials ▶ 2 sheets of Plexiglas™, ¼ or ⅛ inch (.64 or .33 cm) thick and approximately 1 foot (30 cm) square. (Size is not critical.)

▶ 1 piece of dark construction paper.

▶ One 3 × 5 inch (8 × 13 cm) piece of transparent red plastic.

▶ Electrical or duct tape.

▶ A light source, such as a desk lamp.

Assembly
(15 minutes or less)

Peel the paper from the Plexiglas™ and smooth off all edges with sandpaper if necessary. Be careful not to scratch the surfaces. Clean the top and bottom surfaces with alcohol and a soft cloth. Press the plates tightly together and tape around the edges to hold them in place. Tape a sheet of dark construction paper to one plate to make the interference patterns more visible.

To Do and Notice
(15 minutes or more)

Hold the plates, with the dark-paper side on the bottom, in any strong source of white light. Observe the rainbow-colored interference patterns. The patterns will change as you bend, twist, or press on the plates. Notice that the patterns strongly resemble the contour lines on a topographic map.

Place the red plastic between the light source and the plates. Notice that the patterns are now just red and black.

What's Going On?

Light waves reflect from the surfaces of two plastic sheets separated by a thin air gap. These light waves meet after reflecting from the two surfaces. When two waves meet, they can add together, cancel each other, or partially cancel each other. This adding and canceling of light waves, called *constructive interference* and *destructive interference,* creates the rainbow-colored patterns that you see.

White light is made up of all different colors mixed together. When light waves of a particular color meet and cancel each other, that color is subtracted from white light. For example, if the blue light waves cancel, you see what is left of white light after the blue has been removed—yellow (the *complementary color* of blue).

The thickness of the gap between the plates determines which colors of light cancel out at any one point. For example, if the separation of the plates is roughly equal to one-half the wavelength of blue light (or some multiple of it), the crests of waves of blue light reflected from the top surface of the air gap will match up with the troughs of waves reflected from the bottom surface, causing the blue light to cancel out.

This is what happens: Imagine that the distance between the two plates is one-half the wavelength of blue light. When a wave hits the top of the air layer, part reflects and part continues on. Compared to the part that reflects from the top of the air layer, the part that continues on and reflects from the bottom travels an extra wavelength through the air layer (half a wavelength down and half a wavelength back). In addition, the wave that reflects from the bottom is inverted. The net effect is that the blue light waves reflected from the two surfaces recombine trough-to-peak, and cancel each other out.

Because the interference pattern depends on the amount of separation between the plates, what you're actually seeing is a topographical map of the distance between plates.

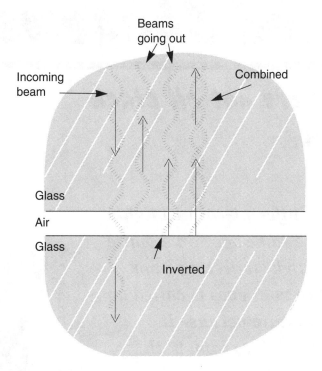

When you place a red filter in front of the light source, only red and black fringes will appear. Where destructive interference takes place, there is no red light left to reach your eyes, so you see black. Where the waves constructively interfere, you see red.

If you can find a sodium-vapor lamp (a yellow street lamp, for example), try placing the plates under its light. The sodium vapor gives off sodium's predominant fingerprint: a very pure yellow light.

The beautiful rainbow colors you see in soap bubbles and on pieces of metal heated to high temperatures are produced in the same way: by light reflecting from the top and bottom of a thin transparent layer.

○ ○ ○ ○ ○ ○ **etc.** ○ ○ ○ ○ ○ ○

When you open a package of new, clean microscope slides, you can often see colored interference patterns created by the thin air space between the glass slides.

Colored Shadows

Shadows are not all black and white.

▶ When two different-colored lights shine on the same spot on a white screen, the light reflecting from that spot to your eyes is called an **additive mixture** *because it contains the colors from both lights. We can learn about human color perception by using colored lights to make additive color mixtures.*

Materials ▶ White surface. (A white wall, white poster-board, or white paper taped to stiff card-board works well. Do not use a beaded or metal slide projection screen.)

▶ Red, green, and blue lightbulbs or flood-lamps, one of each color. Sylvania #11 col-ored lightbulbs or General Electric Dichro-color Dichroic Floodlamps (150 watt) work well. We have even obtained excellent re-sults with clear-colored Christmas tree lights. Smaller or dimmer bulbs are fine for tabletop use by a few students, but larger, brighter bulbs allow a larger-scale demon-stration.

▶ 3 light sockets of any type or arrangement that will get the light from the three bulbs simultaneously directed onto the same area of a white surface.

▶ Any solid object such as a pencil, ruler, cor-rection fluid bottle, finger, etc.

▶ Adult help.

Assembly
(15 minutes or less)

Set up the bulbs and screen in such a way that the light from all three bulbs falls on the same area of the screen and all bulbs are approximately the same distance from the screen. For best re-sults, put the green bulb in between the red and the blue bulbs.

To Do and Notice
(30 minutes or more)

Turn on the lights, and adjust the positions of the bulbs until you obtain the "whitest" light on the area of the screen where the three lights mix. For best results, make the room as dark as possible.

Place a narrow opaque object, like a pencil, fairly close to the screen. Adjust the distance from the screen until you see three distinct colored shadows.

Remove the object, turn off one of the colored lights, and notice how the color on the screen changes. Then replace the object in front of the screen and notice the color of the shadows. Move the object close to the screen until the shadows overlap. Notice the color of these combined shadows.

Repeat the previous step with a different light turned off while the other two remain on, and then a third time so you have tried all combinations. Repeat again with only one color at a time on, and then with all three on. Vary the size of the object and the distance from the screen. Try using your hand as an object.

What's Going On?

The retina of the human eye has three receptors for colored light: One type of receptor is most sensitive to red light, one to green light, and one to blue light. With these three color receptors we are able to perceive more than a million different shades of color.

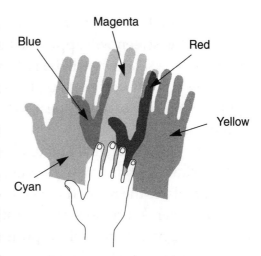

When a red light, a blue light, and a green light are all shining on the screen, the screen looks white because these three colored lights stimulate all three color receptors on your retinas approximately equally, giving us the sensation of white. Red, green, and blue are therefore called *additive primaries* of light.

With these three lights you can make shadows of seven different colors: blue, red, green, black, cyan (blue-green), magenta (a mixture of blue and red), and yellow (a mixture of red and green). If you block two of the three lights, you get a shadow of the third color: Block the red and green lights, for example, and you get a blue shadow. If you block all three lights, you get a black shadow. And if you block one of the three lights, you get a shadow whose color is a mixture of the two other colors. If the blue and green mix, they make cyan; red and blue make magenta; red and green make yellow.

If you turn off the red light, leaving only the blue and green lights on, the lights mix and the screen appears to be cyan, a blue-green color. When you hold the object in front of this cyan screen, you will see two shadows: one blue and one green. In one place the object blocks the light coming from the green bulb and therefore leaves a blue shadow; in another place it blocks the light from the blue bulb to make a green shadow. When you move the object close to the screen you will get a very dark (black) shadow, where the object blocks both lights.

When you turn off the green light, leaving the red and blue lights on, the screen will appear to be magenta, a mixture of red and blue. The shadows will be red and blue.

When you turn off the blue light, leaving the red and green lights on, the screen will appear to be yellow. The shadows will be red and green.

It may seem strange that a red light and a green light mix to make yellow light on a white screen. A mixture of red and green light stimulates the red and green receptors on the retina of your eye. Those same receptors are also stimulated by yellow light—that is, by light from the yellow portion of the rainbow. When the red and green receptors in your eye are stimulated, whether by a mixture of red and green light, or by yellow light alone, you will see the color yellow.

Find out what happens when you use different-colored paper for the screen. Try yellow, green, blue, red, purple, and so on.

If you let light from the three bulbs shine through a hole in a card that is held an appropriate distance from the screen, you will see three separate patches of colored light on the screen, one from each lamp. (Make the hole large enough to get a patch of color you can really see.) If you move the card closer to the screen, the patches of light will eventually overlap and you will see the mixtures of each pair of colors.

Color Table

This Snack will color your perception.

► A colored filter transmits some colors and absorbs others. Using a colored filter, you can decode secret messages written with colored pens or crayons. A brightly colored picture takes on a whole new look when you view it through a colored filter.

Materials ▸ Several different colors of transparent plastic to use as colored filters. (You can use colored acetate report covers, colored acrylic plastic from a plastics store, etc.)

▸ Assorted colored pictures (from magazines, old wall calendars, etc.).

▸ Crayons, colored pencils, or colored pens.

Assembly

No assembly required.

To Do and Notice
(15 minutes or more)

Place one colored filter at a time over a colored picture and notice how the colors are affected. With a red filter, the picture appears entirely in shades of red plus black.

Print your name or a short message on a piece of white paper using a different color of crayon, pencil, or pen for each letter. Then look at the message through a red filter. You may notice that the red letters disappear, but you can still see blue or green letters. By figuring out which colors you still see and which you don't, you can write a secret message and then use the filter as the decoder.

What's Going On?

An ideal red filter transmits only red light and absorbs all other colors. In this ideal case, a picture containing red, green, and blue would appear red and black when viewed through a red filter.

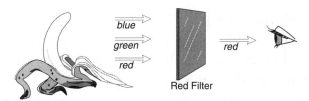

A red filter blocks green light and blue light: Only red light can get through to your eyes. The white banana and the yellow peel both reflect some red light, so the whole banana looks red.

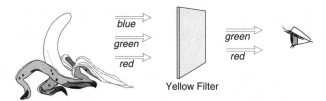

A yellow filter blocks blue light, so only red light and green light can get to your eyes. The white banana and the yellow peel both reflect some green light and some red light. The whole banana looks yellow because green light plus red light mix to make yellow light.

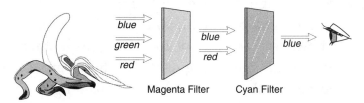

Here, a magenta filter blocks green light and a cyan filter blocks red light. Only blue light can pass through to your eyes. The banana looks blue because the white fruit reflects some blue light. But the yellow peel looks black. It reflects no blue light.

Likewise, a pure blue filter transmits only blue light, and a pure green filter transmits only green light. Any color from a picture that is not transmitted by the filter will be absorbed by the filter and will not be seen.

In reality, most filters are not ideal filters. That is, a filter might transmit primarily green, but also some blue. Since most filters are not ideal, most pictures will not appear as strictly one color and black.

When you view multicolored writing through an ideal red

filter, only red light reaches your eyes. Red light comes from both the red letters and the white paper (since white contains all colors). The red letters tend to disappear, since they blend right in with the red light from the white paper. Letters that contain no red would appear black. Since most pigments are not perfectly pure, you may notice that more than just the red letters blend in with the background. That is, if a yellow letter reflects red (since yellow light can be made from a combination of red light and green light) the yellow letter would blend in with the background.

Magazine illustrations are colored with pigments, but when you look at the illustration, you are sensing the light that is being reflected to your eyes. The following information about light and pigments may help you better understand what you see when you look at a colored illustration through a filter.

Most colors of light can be made by mixing three primary colors of light: red light, blue light, and green light. Most colors of pigments, however, can be made by mixing magenta, cyan, and yellow pigments. Magenta pigment reflects red and blue light. More important, it absorbs, or subtracts, green light. Cyan pigment subtracts red light. Yellow pigment subtracts blue light. Four-color printing in magazines is done with inks of these three colors—magenta, cyan, and yellow—plus black. Mixed properly, these pigments produce the entire range of colors found in colored pictures in magazines.

A related Snack dealing with combinations of color is *Colored Shadows.*

Corner Reflector

See yourself as others see you.

▶ Two hinged mirrors create a kaleidoscope that shows multiple images of an object. The number of images depends on the angle between the mirrors. When you set the hinged mirrors on top of a third mirror, you create a reflector that always sends light back in the direction from which it came.

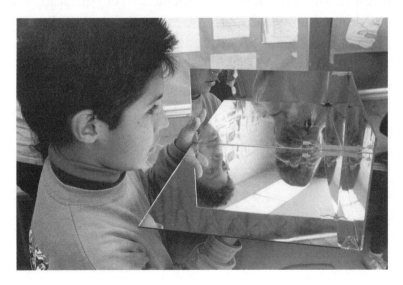

Materials ▸ Three 6 × 6 inch (15 × 15 cm) mirrors. Plastic mirrors are best, since there is less danger of breaking the mirror or cutting your fingers. Plastic mirrors are available at plastics supply stores and can easily be cut to any size. Glass mirror tiles are readily available but are not as safe.

▸ Duct tape.

▸ A piece of light cardboard (such as a manila file folder).

▸ Adult help.

Assembly
(30 minutes or less)

If you start with one large piece of mirror, cut three 6 × 6 inch (15 × 15 cm) pieces from the plastic or glass. You can cut the plastic with a fine saw, such as a hacksaw, or score it with a utility knife and then snap it off. It is not hard to cut glass; get someone who knows how to do it to show you. (WARNING: For safety,

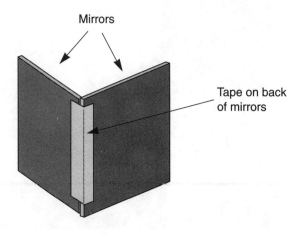

Mirrors

Tape on back of mirrors

after cutting a glass mirror, mount it on wood or cardboard and cover the edges with duct tape.)

Once you have the three mirrors you need, use the duct tape to tape two of the mirrors together along one edge. Put the tape on the back side of the mirror, making a hinge that opens and closes easily. Be sure the mirrors can move freely from 0 degrees to 180 degrees.

To Do and Notice
(15 minutes or more)

To make a kaleidoscope, set the hinged mirrors on the cardboard, and place an object such as a pencil or some coins between them. Open the mirrors to different angles. Notice that the smaller the angle, the greater the number of images you see. Remove the objects and see what happens when you draw different designs in the space between the two mirrors.

Close your right eye and look at a single mirror straight on. Notice that the left eye of the image is closed. Now close your right eye and look at two mirrors that form a 90-degree angle. Notice that the right eye of this image is closed.

Now make a corner reflector by opening the two taped mirrors to 90 degrees and resting them on the third mirror, so that the three mirrors form a half cube (see diagram). Close one eye and stare right at the corner where the three mirrors join. Move your head and notice that the pupil of your open eye always falls right at the corner. Open both eyes and look at the corner. One eye may appear to be closer to the corner than the other. This is your dominant eye.

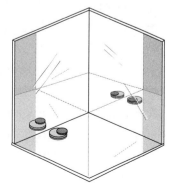

What's Going On?

When you put an object between the two hinged mirrors, light from the object bounces back and forth between the mirrors before it reaches your eyes. An image is formed each time the light bounces off a mirror. The number of images that you see in the mirrors depends on the angle that the mirrors form. As you make the angle between the mirrors smaller, the light bounces back and forth more times, and you see more images.

The illustration below shows how an image is formed in the corner of two mirrors at 90 degrees. Light rays bounce off each mirror at the same angle that they hit the mirror: Physicists say that the *angle of reflection* is equal to the *angle of incidence.* Mirrors at other angles behave similarly, but the ray diagrams may get more complex.

The inside corner of a corner reflector (where the three mirrors meet) sends light back parallel to its original path. If you pointed a thin beam of laser light right near the corner, the beam would bounce from mirror to mirror and then exit parallel to the entering beam. Light from the center of your eye bounces straight back to the center of your eye, so the image of your eye seems to be centered in the corner made by the mirrors.

In a corner reflector, multiple reflections reverse the image and invert it.

○ ○ ○ ○ ○ ○ **etc.** ○ ○ ○ ○ ○ ○

Corner reflectors are used to make safety reflectors for cars, bicycles, and signs. Corner reflectors have also been used to bounce laser beams back to the earth from the surface of the moon.

Throw a tennis ball into the corner of a room. It should return to you after bouncing off the three surfaces.

Tape five square mirrors together with the mirrored surfaces facing inward to form a box. Place a sixth mirror, turned at a 45-degree angle, over the open side so you can look into the box and also let some light in. This combines the _Look into Infinity_ Snack with this _Corner Reflector_ Snack. Try other configurations of mirrors in three dimensions and see what you can discover.

To do a quantitative experiment, mark the following angles on a piece of cardboard: 180 degrees, 90 degrees, 60 degrees, 45 degrees, 36 degrees, 30 degrees, and 20 degrees. These angles are chosen so that when they are divided into 360 degrees they produce an even integer. Mount the hinged mirrors at each of these angles and place an object between them. Count the number of images you see. You should be able to verify the following rule: 360 divided by the angle between the mirrors gives the number of images, plus one. At 60 degrees, for example, 360/60 = 6, so you should see five images of the object.

Critical Angle

Why your phone calls don't leak out of optical fibers.

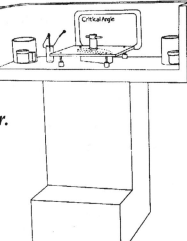

▶ A transparent material such as glass or water can actually reflect light better than any mirror. All you have to do is look at it from the proper angle.

Materials ► A light source with a well-defined beam. A laser is best, if one is available. Otherwise, you can use a Mini-Maglite® flashlight focused to make a beam, or a slide projector with its beam narrowed. (To narrow the beam of a slide projector, cut an index card the same size as a slide, and then make a hole in the middle of it with a paper hole-punch. Put it in the projector so the light only goes through the hole.)

► A rectangular aquarium filled with water.

► A few drops of milk (or some powdered milk) to add to the aquarium water to make the beam visible.

Assembly
(15 minutes or less)

Fill the aquarium with water. Then add the milk a drop at a time, stirring after each drop, until you can see the light beam pass through the water. If you use powdered milk, add a pinch at a time.

To Do and Notice
(15 minutes or more)

Direct the light beam upward through the water so that it hits the surface of the water from underneath. You can shine the beam into the water through the transparent bottom of the aquarium, or in through the side wall. (With the Mini-Maglite®,

you can seal the light in a
watertight plastic bag and
place the light right in the
water.) The beam will be
more visible if you can dim
the room lights.

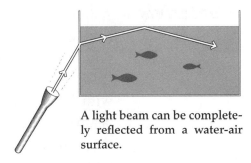

A light beam can be completely reflected from a water-air
surface.

Point the beam so that
it hits the surface of the wa-
ter at just about a right angle. In the aquarium, you may be able
to see both the *reflected* beam, which bounces back into the water, and the *refracted* beam, which comes out of the water and into
the air. (Dust in the air helps you see the refracted beam. You can
add chalk dust to the air. You can also search for the beam and
track it with a piece of paper.) Notice that most of the beam
leaves the water and only a faint beam is reflected back down
into the water.

Slowly change the angle at which the beam of light hits the
surface of the water. Notice that the beam reflected into the water grows brighter as the beam transmitted into the air becomes
dimmer. Also notice that the transmitted beam is bent, or refracted.

Experiment until you find the angle at which the transmitted
beam completely disappears. At this angle, called the *critical angle*, all of the light is reflected back into the water.

What's Going On?

In general, when a beam of light (the *incident beam*) hits the interface between two transparent materials, such as air and water, part of the beam is reflected and part of it continues through
the interface and on into the other material. The light beam is
bent, or refracted, as it passes from one material into the next.

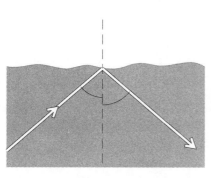 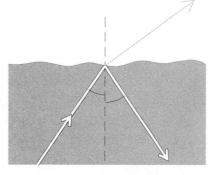

When the angles marked are greater than 49°, light is totally reflected from a water-air surface.

When the angles marked are less than 49°, some light leaves the water.

The farther the beam is from perpendicular when it hits the surface, the more strongly it is bent. If the light is moving from a material with a low speed of light into a material with a higher speed of light (for example, from water into air), the bending is toward the surface. At some angle, the bending will be so strong that the refracted beam will be directed right along the surface; that is, none of it will get out into the air.

Beyond that angle (the critical angle), all the light is reflected back into the water, so the reflected beam is as bright as the incident beam. This phenomenon is called *total internal reflection,* because very nearly 100% of the beam is reflected, which is better than the very best mirror surfaces.

The critical angle for water is measured between the beam and a line perpendicular to the surface, and is 49 degrees.

○ ○ ○ ○ ○ ○ ○ **etc.** ○ ○ ○ ○ ○ ○

Total internal reflection helps transmit telephone messages along optical fibers. Any light that is not aligned parallel to the axis of the fiber hits the wall of the fiber and is reflected (totally!) back inward,

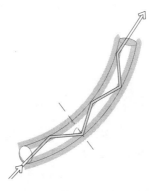

since the angle of incidence with which the light hits
the wall is much larger than the critical angle. This
helps prevent the signal from weakening too rapidly
over long distances, or from leaking out when the
fiber goes around a curve.

This demonstration can also be done by replacing
the aquarium and water with a small transparent
plastic block, which can be bought at a local plastics
supply store. Such blocks are also available as part of
the Blackboard Optics™ set made by Klinger Scientific.

Cylindrical Mirror

This cylindrical mirror lets you see yourself as others see you.

▶ A flat mirror will always reflect an image that is right-side up and reversed right to left. A cylindrical mirror can produce images that are flipped upside down and images that are not reversed. The image you see in a cylindrical mirror depends on the orientation of the mirror and the distance between you and the mirror.

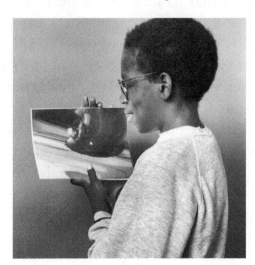

Materials ▸ One 8½ × 11 inch (22 × 28 cm) sheet of aluminized Mylar™.

▸ 1 transparent page protector (available in stationery stores).

▸ Construction paper or other stiff paper backing.

Assembly
(5 minutes or less)

Put the stiff paper backing behind the Mylar™ and slide them both into the transparent page protector. Bend the Mylar™ to form a portion of a cylinder. When you bend the Mylar™, be sure that the long side is parallel to the axis of the cylinder.

To Do and Notice
(15 minutes ore more)

Hold the cylindrical mirror so that its long axis is horizontal. Curve the Mylar™ slightly and look into the mirror. Position yourself so that you can clearly see a reflection of your face. Notice how the image changes when you move closer to or farther from the mirror. When you move far enough away from the mirror, your image will flip upside down.

Wink your right eye. Which eye does the image wink? The image may wink its left eye or its right eye, depending on how far your face is from the mirror. When you are close to the mirror and your image is right-side up, the image winks its left eye. When it is upside down, the image winks its right eye. (If you have trouble deciding which eye the image is winking, have someone stand beside the mirror and do what the image does—that is, wink the same eye as the image. Then ask your partner if he or she is winking the right or left eye. If the image is upside down, your partner will have to turn upside down, too. Your partner can bend over at the waist and look at you between the legs.)

Now orient the cylindrical mirror so that its long axis is vertical. Notice how the image changes when you move closer to and farther from the mirror. Wink your right eye and notice how the image in the mirror responds. When you are close, the image will wink its left eye. When you are far away, it will wink its right eye.

What's Going On?

You see the world because light gets into your eyes. You see these words, for example, because light reflecting from this page enters your eyes and makes an image on your retina.

When you make a visual picture of the world, you assume that the light entering your eyes has traveled in a straight line to reach you. But mirrors and other shiny objects change the path

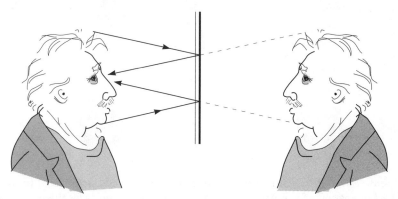

Light from your hair bounces off the mirror and enters your eyes from above; light from your chin enters your eyes from below.

of the light, bouncing it back in an organized fashion. When you look into a mirror, you see your image because light reflecting from your face bounces off the mirror and back into your eyes. Your eyes and brain assume that the light has traveled in a straight line to reach your eyes, so you see an image of your face out there in front of or behind the mirror.

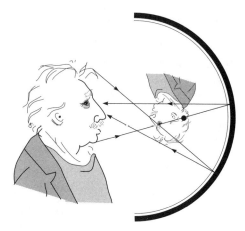

The light bouncing from a curved mirror makes an inverted image.

What you see in a mirror depends on how the light bounces off the mirror and into your eyes. When light hits a mirror, it bounces off in the same way that a ball would bounce off the mirror. If you threw a ball straight at a flat mirror, it would bounce straight back. If the mirror was curved so that the ball struck the surface at an angle, it would bounce away at an angle.

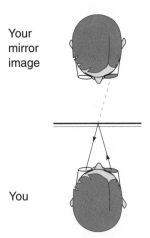

Your mirror image

You

Light scattered by your right eye bounces off a flat mirror in the same way a ball would bounce off the mirror.

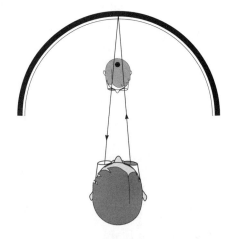

In a concave curved mirror, light from the right (east) eye bounces off the mirror and forms an image of an eye on the right (west) side of the face in the mirror.

When you look into an ordinary flat mirror, the image of your face is right side up: Your hair is on top of your head and your chin is underneath. To reach your eyes, the light from your hair hits the mirror at a slight angle and then bounces into your eyes from above—which is why you see your hair on top and your image as right side up.

When you look into a cylindrical mirror with the axis of the mirror horizontal and with your face a foot or more away from the mirror, your image is upside down. That's because the light from your hair bounces off the curved mirror and comes to your eyes from below.

To make sense of the angle at which the light is entering your eyes, your eyes and brain must see the image of your face as upside down and a little bit in front of the mirror.

As everyone knows, a flat mirror reverses your right side and your left side. How does it do that? Suppose you are standing face to face with another person. If your right ear points toward the east, his or her left ear will point toward the east. Now, instead of facing another person, suppose you are facing a flat mirror with your right ear pointing to the east. The light from your right ear will bounce off the flat mirror and enter your eyes from the east. Even though your east ear is the east ear of the image, your right ear has become the left ear of the image! (Yes, this is a little mind-boggling at first reading. But once you get it, it will seem simple.)

Now look into the cylindrical mirror with its axis vertical. Stand at least a foot away from the mirror. Once again, place your right ear so that it points to the east. Light from your right ear bounces off the curved mirror and enters your eyes from the west. Light from your right ear appears to come from the right ear of the image. In this cylindrical mirror, you see yourself as others see you. You see the image of your face just a little bit in front of the mirror.

○ ○ ○ ○ ○ ○   **etc.**   ○ ○ ○ ○ ○ ○

Here's a classic tricky question: "If a flat mirror reverses right and left, why doesn't it reverse up and down?"

The answer is that a flat mirror actually reverses in and out. That is, light that travels "in" to the mirror is bounced back "out" of the mirror. This reversal does not change up into down, but it does change right into left. Consider the outline of the hand below. Is it a right hand or a left hand? You cannot tell which hand it is unless you know whether the palm of the hand is facing "in" to the page or "out" of the page. So right and left depend on in and out.

This hand is either right or left, depending on which way the palm is facing.

Diffraction

Light can bend around edges.

▶ Light bends when it passes around an edge or through a slit. This bending is called **diffraction**. You can easily demonstrate diffraction using a candle or a small bright flashlight bulb and a slit made with two pencils. The **diffraction pattern**, *the pattern of dark and light created when light bends around an edge or edges, shows that light has wavelike properties.*

Materials ▸ 2 clean new pencils.

▸ A piece of transparent tape. (Any thin tape will do.)

▸ A candle.

or

▸ A Mini-Maglite® flashlight (available for under $15 in many hardware stores). Do not substitute other flashlights.

or

▸ A flashlight bulb for a Mini-Maglite®, two AA batteries, a battery holder (available from Radio Shack), and two clip leads.

▸ Optional: pieces of cloth, a feather, plastic diffraction grating, a metal screen, a human hair.

Assembly
(5 minutes or less)

Light the candle or, if you are using a Mini-Maglite®, unscrew the top of the flashlight. The tiny lamp will come on and shine brightly. You can also make your own bright point source of light by attaching the Mini-Maglite® flashlight bulb to the battery holder with the clip leads. Be sure you put two AA batteries in the battery holder.

Wrap one layer of tape around the top of one of the pencils, just below the eraser.

To Do and Notice
(15 minutes or more)

If you measure distances on the diffraction pattern, you can calculate the wavelength of light emitted by the candle or bulb.

Place the light at least one arm-length away from you.

Hold the two pencils vertically, side by side, with the erasers at the top. The tape wrapped around one pencil should keep the pencils slightly apart, forming a thin slit between them, just below the tape. Hold the pencils close to one eye (about 1 inch [2.5 cm] away) and look at the light source through the slit between the pencils. Squeeze the pencils together, making the slit smaller. Notice that there is a line of light perpendicular to the slit. While looking through the slit, rotate the pencils until they are horizontal, and notice that the line of light becomes vertical.

If you look closely you may see that the line is composed of tiny blobs of light. As you squeeze the slit together, the blobs of light grow larger and spread apart, moving away from the central light source and becoming easier to see. Notice that the blobs have blue and red edges and that the blue edges are closer to the light source.

Stretch a hair tight and hold it about 1 inch (2.5 cm) from your eye. Move the hair until it is between your eye and the light source, and notice that the light is spread into a line of blobs by the hair, just as it was by the slit. Rotate the hair and watch the line of blobs rotate.

Look at the light through a piece of cloth, a feather, a diffraction grating, or a piece of metal screen. Rotate each object while you look through it.

What's Going On?

The black bands between the blobs of light show that there is a wave associated with the light. The light waves that go through the slit spread out, overlap, and add together, interacting in complex ways to produce the diffraction pattern that you see. Where the crest of one wave overlaps with the crest of another wave, the two waves combine to make a bigger wave, and you see a bright blob of light. Where the trough of one wave overlaps with the crest of another wave, the waves cancel one another out, and you see a dark band.

The angle at which the light bends is proportional to the wavelength of the light. Red light, for instance, has a longer wavelength than blue light, and so it bends more than blue light does. This different amount of bending gives the blobs their colored edges: blue on the inside, red on the outside.

The narrower the slit, the more the light spreads out. In fact, the angle between two adjacent dark bands in the diffraction pattern is inversely proportional to the width of the slit.

Thin objects, such as a strand of hair, also diffract light. Light that passes around the hair spreads out, overlaps, and produces a diffraction pattern. A piece of cloth or a feather, which are both made up of many smaller, thinner parts, produce complicated diffraction patterns.

○ ○ ○ ○ ○ ○ **etc.** ○ ○ ○ ○ ○ ○

In a dimly lit room, look at a Mini-Maglite® bulb with one eye (a candle will not work). Notice the lines of light radiating out from the light source, like the seeds radiating out from the center of a dandelion. Propose experiments to find the origin of these lines. For example, rotate the light source, and notice that the lines of light do not rotate. Rotate your head, and notice that the lines do rotate. Hold your hand or an index card in front of your eye so that it doesn't quite block

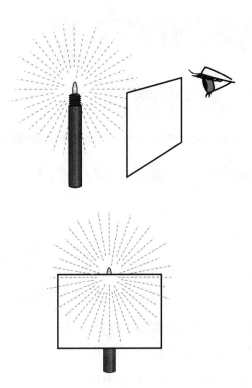

your view of the light source. Notice that you still see a full circle of lines radiating out from the light source. The lines of light are spread out onto your retina by imperfections in the tissues of your cornea.

Disappearing Glass Rods

You can make glass objects disappear.

▶ Glass objects are visible because
they reflect some of the light that
shines on them and bend or refract
the light that shines through them.
If you eliminate reflection from
and refraction by a glass object,
you can make that object disappear.

Materials ▸ Wesson™ oil. (Regular, not lite.)

▸ One or more Pyrex® stirring rods or other small, clear glass objects.

▸ A beaker.

▸ Optional: glass eyedropper, glass magnifying lens.

Assembly
(1 minute or less)

Pour some Wesson™ oil into the beaker.

To Do and Notice
(15 minutes or more)

Immerse a glass object in the oil. Notice that the object becomes more difficult to see. Only a ghostly image of the object remains. If you do this as a demonstration, keep your audience at a distance to make it harder for them to see the ghost object.

Experiment with a variety of glass objects, such as clear marbles, lenses, and odd glassware. Some will disappear in the oil more completely than others.

You can make an eyedropper vanish before your eyes by immersing it and then sucking oil up into the dropper.

Immerse the magnifying lens in the oil. Notice that it does not magnify images when it is submerged.

What's Going On?

When light traveling through air encounters a glass surface at an angle, some of the light *reflects*. The rest of the light keeps going, but it bends or *refracts* as it moves from the air to the glass. You see a glass object because it both reflects and refracts light.

When light passes from air into glass, it slows down. It's this change in speed that causes the light to reflect and refract as it moves from one clear material (air) to another (glass). Every material has an *index of refraction* that is linked to the speed of light in the material. The higher a material's index of refraction, the slower light travels in that material.

The smaller the difference in speed between two clear materials, the less reflection will occur at the boundary and the less refraction will occur for the transmitted light. If a transparent object is surrounded by another material that has the same index of refraction, then the speed of light will not change as it enters the object. No reflection and no refraction will take place, and the object will be invisible.

Wesson™ oil has nearly the same index of refraction (n) as Pyrex® glass ($n = 1.474$). Different glasses have different indices of refraction. In Wesson™ oil, Pyrex® disappears, but other types of glass—such as crown glass or flint glass—remain visible. Fortunately for us, a great deal of laboratory glassware and home kitchen glassware is made from Pyrex® glass.

For most Pyrex® glass, the index matching with Wesson™ oil is not perfect. This is because the Pyrex® glass has internal strains that make its index of refraction vary at different places in the object. Even if you can match the index of refraction for one part of a Pyrex® stirring rod, the match will not be perfect for other parts of the rod. That's why a ghostly image of the rod remains even with the best index matching.

The index of refraction of the oil (and of the glass, too) is a function of temperature. This demonstration will work better on some days than others.

 **etc.**

Index of refraction is sometimes called *optical density,* but optical density is not the same as *mass density.* Two materials can have different mass densities even when they have the same index of refraction. Though Pyrex® glass and Wesson™ oil have similar indices of refraction, Pyrex® sinks in Wesson™ oil because it has a higher mass density than the oil. Wesson™ oil has a higher index of refraction than water ($n = 1.33$), but it has a lower mass density and floats on water. The index of refraction depends not only on density, but also on the chemical composition of a material.

You can also make Pyrex® glass disappear by immersing it in mineral oil, which is available from pharmacies or chemical supply houses. However, mineral oil comes in light, medium, and heavy weights, and each variety has a different index of refraction. To match the index of refraction of Pyrex® glass, you'll need a mixture of mineral oils of different weights. To create the proper mixture, place a Pyrex® glass object into a large glass beaker and pour in enough heavy mineral oil to submerge it partially. Slowly add light mineral oil and stir. Watch the glass object as you pour.

Most Pyrex® glass will disappear when the mixture is about 2 parts heavy mineral oil to 1 part light mineral oil. Notice the swirling refraction patterns as you mix the two oils.

Karo™ syrup is another material that has an index of refraction close to that of glass. Karo™ can be diluted with water to match some varieties of glass.

Duck into Kaleidoscope

Make multiple images of yourself.

▶ Duck into Kaleidoscope *will create hundreds of images of whatever you place inside it. The basic kaleidoscope is a triangle, but mirror tiles can be formed into other shapes and angles as well.*

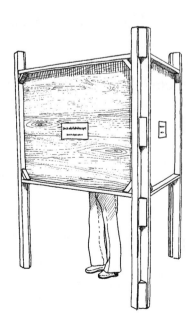

Materials ▸ 6 mirror tiles measuring 1 × 1 foot (30 × 30 cm). (Or use plastic mirrors from a plastic supply house.)

▸ Duct tape.

▸ 3 pieces of sturdy cardboard measuring 1 × 2 feet (30 × 60 cm).

▸ Adult help.

Assembly
(30 minutes or less)

Place the six mirror tiles in a row, as shown below. Tape each tile to the tiles on either side with duct tape, leaving just enough room for the tape to flex and act as a hinge. Tape over any sharp edges.

Stand the pieces of cardboard on a table so that the long sides are horizontal. Fold the bottom 3 inches (7.5 cm) of each piece of cardboard to form a lip. Tape the 3 cardboard pieces together to form a large equilateral triangle (2 feet [60 cm] on each side), with the lip on the inside.

Form the mirror tiles into an equilateral triangle that is 2 feet (60 cm) on each side, and insert them into the cardboard form so that the bottom edges of the mirrors rest in the cardboard lip. (Be sure that the mirrors are facing inside.)

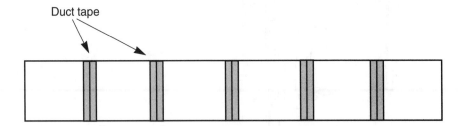

Duct tape

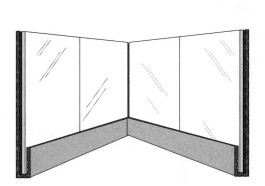
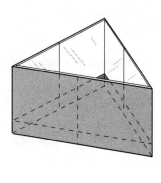

To Do and Notice
(5 minutes or more)

Put the kaleidoscope over your head. You will see a million faces!

Take the mirrors out of the cardboard form and make them into various closed geometrical shapes, such as a square, a rectangle, or a hexagon. Put each shape over your head, or place an object in the center of the shape, and see the reflections.

What's Going On?

In a kaleidoscope you see reflections of reflections.

○ ○ ○ ○ ○ ○ **etc.** ○ ○ ○ ○ ○ ○

Related Snacks: *Corner Reflector* and *Look into Infinity.*

Giant Lens

A lens creates an image that hangs in midair.

▶ A large hanging lens creates upside-down images of distant objects and right-side-up images of nearby objects. You can locate the upside-down images by using a piece of white paper as a screen. The right-side-up images are harder to find.

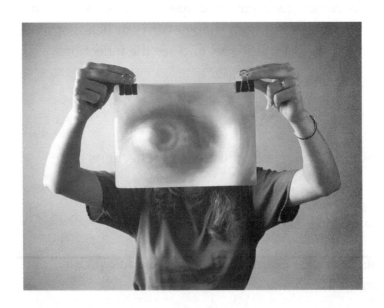

Materials ► A large plastic page-magnifier Fresnel lens (6 × 9 inches [15 × 22 cm] or larger). Be sure you don't get a wide-angle viewer lens. If you look through the lens at a hand held an inch or so beyond the lens, the hand should appear larger, not smaller.

► Spring clips from a stationery store. (See drawing.)

► Corrugated cardboard or foamcore sheet, 9 × 9 inches (22 × 22 cm).

► 2 soda straws.

► Common pins.

► String.

► A partner.

Assembly
(5 minutes or less)

Hang the lens from the ceiling at about head height using the clips and string, or use the clips to support the lens on a table-top, as shown in the drawing.

To Do and Notice
(30 minutes or more)

Stand a few feet back from the lens and look through it at objects on the other side. Distant objects will appear upside down; near-by objects will appear right-side up.

Stand close to the lens. Hold your hand close to the lens on

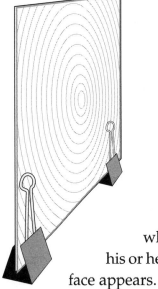

the other side. You will notice that your hand is magnified and right side up.

Stand an arm's length from one side of the lens; have a friend stand an arm's length from the other side. Look at your friend's face through the lens. Have your friend bring his or her face closer to the lens as you back away, keeping the same two-arms' length distance between the two of you. Then reverse this procedure: You step closer to the lens while he or she moves away. Notice how his or her face appears; ask your friend how your face appears.

Find an object that is brightly illuminated (such as a light-bulb or a computer screen), and dim the lights in the rest of the room. Hold the lens at least several feet from the object. Hold a large piece of white paper against the side of the lens that faces away from the object. Slowly move the paper away from the lens until an image of the object comes into focus on the paper.

What's Going On?

Light from any point on an object spreads out in all directions. When the spreading light hits the page-magnifier lens, it is bent toward the axis of the lens. (The page magnifier is called a positive, or converging, lens because it bends light rays together.)

Page magnifiers have a *focal length* of about 10 inches (25 cm). A focal length is the distance from the lens to an image the lens makes of a distant object. If an object is farther than one focal length (10 inches [25 cm]) from the lens, the lens can bend all the light that arrives from one point on the object until it comes back to a point on the other side of the lens. This point is a point on

the image of the object. If you put white paper at the place where the light rays meet, an image will appear on the paper. An image that can be focused on a piece of paper is called a *real image*. (See Figure 1 on page 58.)

However, you don't need the white paper to see the image. Simply move about 1 foot (30 cm) farther away from the lens than the location of the image, and look at the lens. You will see the image hanging in space. Move your head slightly from side to side and watch the image move. (Actually, your eye-brain system may refuse to interpret the image as hanging in the air. It is so unusual to see something hanging in the air that your brain may insist that the image is on the surface of the lens or even behind the lens—however, the image is actually hanging in space.)

If an object is closer to the lens than the focal point, the lens cannot bend the light spreading from the object enough to return it to a point. To your eye-brain system, it looks like there is an image on the same side of the lens as the object. This type of image is called a *virtual image.* It cannot be focused on a piece of paper. (See Figure 2 on page 58.)

You can find the location of a real or virtual image by building an image locator. Push a pin through one end of each soda

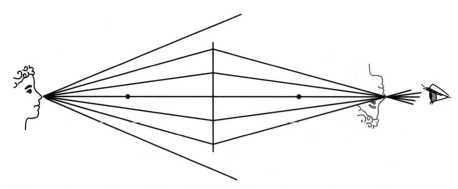

Figure 1. Your eye-brain follows the light back to the point from which it spreads. This type of image is called a *real image*.

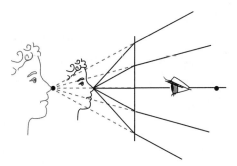

Figure 2. Your eye-brain follows the light back to the point from which it appears to spread. This type of image is called a *virtual image*.

straw. Use the pins to attach the straws to adjacent corners of the 9 × 9 inch (22 × 22 cm) corrugated cardboard sheet. Push another pin through the other end of one straw to mount it along one edge of the cardboard. The other straw will be free to rotate.

Mount the image locator firmly in place so that you can look through the straw fixed to one edge and see one point on the image (see the diagram at the top of page 59). Then rotate the other straw until you can look through it and see the same point on the image. (You'll have to move your head to look through the second straw.) The image is located where two imaginary lines, one drawn through each straw, cross. If the image is a real image, you can place a piece of paper there and see it on the paper.

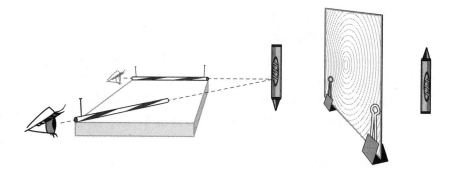

○ ○ ○ ○ ○ ○ **etc.** ○ ○ ○ ○ ○ ○

You can find the focal length of your particular lens using a bright light source that is more than 30 feet (9 m) away. (CAUTION: Don't use the sun! The image you make can become so hot that it can burn the paper, and so bright that it can damage your eyes.) Hold a piece of paper against the lens on the side opposite the light. Move the paper away from the lens until a sharp image of the light appears on the paper. The distance from the lens to the image is the *focal length.*

This type of lens is called a *Fresnel lens,* after August Fresnel, who figured out how to make these lenses for the French lighthouse commission in the late 1800s. Lighthouses needed large lenses to gather the

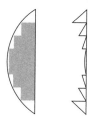

light from a lamp and make it into a beam. If such a lens were ground out of glass, it would be thick, heavy, and expensive. Fresnel realized that the bending of light at the lens occurred at its curved surface, and that the thick glass had a minimal role in image formation. He figured out a way to maintain the curvature of the surface while getting rid of the useless glass. He made his lighthouse lenses out of prisms.

The plastic lenses we have used are made out of wedges of plastic. The wedges must be thicker at the edge in order to bend light more, and thinner in the center. Run your finger over the ridges of the Fresnel lens and notice that the ridges are higher near the edge and lower and smoother near the center.

Inverse Square Law

Why the world gets dark so fast outside the circle of the campfire.

▶ We all know that a light, such as a candle or a streetlight, looks dimmer the farther away from it we get. The question of how much dimmer it looks was answered a long time ago. Here's an easy way to repeat that discovery.

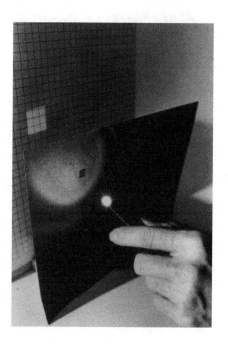

Version 1: Graph Paper Version

Materials
- ▶ A Mini-Maglite® flashlight. No substitutes! A point source of light is required for this Snack. (Or make your own economical light source with a square of heavy cardboard, a Mini-Maglite® replacement bulb, two batteries—either AAA, AA, C, or D—and clip leads to connect them. See Assembly for details.)

- ▶ Cardboard or foamcore.

- ▶ A file card.

- ▶ A knife or scissors.

- ▶ Graph paper with ½ inch (12 mm) or ¼ inch (6 mm) squares.

- ▶ Adult help.

Version 2: Perfboard Version

Materials
- ▶ Perfboard (available at Radio Shack).

- ▶ A file card.

- ▶ Cardboard to use as a screen.

- ▶ A knife or scissors.

- ▶ A pencil.

- ▶ Adult help.

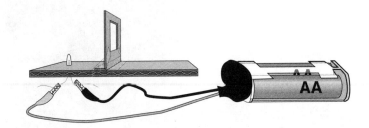

Graph Paper Version
Assembly
(5 minutes or less if you use a Mini-Maglite®; 30 minutes or less if you make the light source)

Unscrew the front reflector assembly of the Mini-Maglite® to expose the bulb. The bulb on the Mini-Maglite® will come on and stay on when the reflector assembly is removed.

If you're making your own light source, you need a replacement bulb for the Mini-Maglite®, two batteries (either AAA, AA, C, or D), and clip leads to connect them. Using the clip leads, wire the bulb in series with the batteries (see the diagram on page 62). Cut a small hole in the cardboard. Push the bulb through the hole so that it fights tightly and gives you something to hold on to.

Now cut a ½ × ½ inch (1.3 × 1.3 cm) square hole in the file card. Hold or mount the card 1 inch (2.5 cm) in front of the light source. The square of light made when the light shines through this hole will shine on the graph paper.

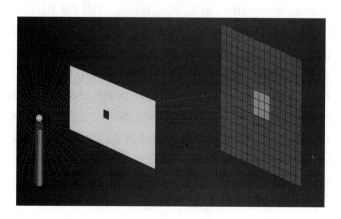

To Do and Notice
(15 minutes or more)

Keep the distance between the bulb and the card with the square hole constant at 1 inch (2.5 cm). Put the graph paper at different distances from the bulb, and count how many squares on the graph paper are lit at each distance. The results will be easier to understand if you make a table of "number of squares lit" versus "distance." Be sure to measure the distance from the bulb.

What's Going On?

The light from the Mini-Maglite® spreads out equally in all directions. As the distance from the bulb to the graph paper increases, the same amount of light spreads over a larger and larger area, and the light reaching each square becomes correspondingly less intense. For example, adjust the distance from the bulb to the graph paper to 1 inch (2.5 cm). At this distance, the graph paper touches the card. A single ½ inch (1.3 cm) square area will be illuminated. When the graph paper is moved 2 inches (5 cm) from the card, four ½ inch (1.3 cm) squares will be illuminated on the graph paper. When the graph paper is moved 3 inches (8 cm) from the card, 9 squares will be illuminated. At 4 inches (10 cm), 16 squares will be illuminated, and so on. The area illuminated will increase as the square of the distance.

The intensity of light is the power per area. Since the energy that comes through the hole you cut is spread out over a larger area, the intensity of light decreases. Since the area increases as the square of the distance, the intensity of the light must decrease as the inverse square of the distance. Thus, intensity follows the *inverse-square law.*

Perfboard Version

Assembly
(30 minutes or less)

Follow the instructions for the light source in the Assembly instructions on page 63. Tape a piece of perfboard to the card. Perfboard is a thin board drilled with holes 1/10 inch (2 mm) apart. Cut a hole in a card so that light shines through a square area 8 holes wide and 8 holes long making 64 points of light. Hold a second card touching the perfboard, and with your pencil draw a square around the 64 points of light.

To Do and Notice
(15 minutes or more)

Mount the perfboard 1 inch (2.5 cm) from the bulb. Hold the second square different distances from the bulb and record the number of points of light that fall in the square. At 1 inch (2.5 cm), all 64 holes fit within the square. At 2 inches (5 cm), 16 points fall within the square.

What's Going On?

The number of points of light is proportional to the inverse square of the distance: it follows the inverse-square law as explained above. You can also do this experiment with a piece of perfboard that has 32 holes across and 32 holes vertically. It will make 1,000 points of light.

The inverse-square law applies not only to the intensity of light, but also to gravitational and electrical forces. The pull of the earth's gravity drops off at $1/r^2$, where r is the distance from the center of the earth. The attraction or repulsion between two electric charges decreases with the distance at $1/r^2$, where r is the distance between the two charges.

Look into Infinity

Images of images of images can repeat forever.

▶ If you have ever been between two mirrors that face each other, such as in a barber shop or a beauty salon, you will be familiar with the seemingly endless line of images fading into the distance. The **Look into Infinity** *Snack* recreates this effect.

Materials ► 2 square pieces of plexi-mirror measuring 12 × 12 inches (30 × 30 cm). (Available from plastics stores. Mirror size is not crucial. You can substitute a 12 × 12 inch [30 × 30 cm] glass mirror tile or any two mirrors for the plexi-mirror. See To Do and Notice.)

► Some kind of stand. (See Assembly.)

► Adult help.

Assembly
(15 minutes or less)

Cut a hole about 1 inch (2.5 cm) in diameter near the center of one of the mirrors. You can use a hole saw, or you can have this done for you at the plastics store. You can get the effect without the hole, but the hole gives a more interesting perspective. If you don't care about the hole, you can use glass mirror tiles instead of a plexi-mirror. You can even create the hole on a glass mirror tile by scraping away the silver backing.

Stand the mirrors so that their reflecting surfaces face each other and are parallel to each other. The mirrors can be anywhere from a few inches to a foot apart. You can make a wooden stand for each mirror by cutting a slit along the length of the flat side of a piece of 1 × 4 inch (2.5 × 10 cm) pine. Then slip the mirror into the slit. You can also stand each mirror between two pieces of wood held together by rubber bands, or place two full soft-drink cans (or any heavy objects) so that one is on each side of the mirror, supporting it.

To Do and Notice
(5 minutes or more)

With the reflecting surfaces facing each other, look through the hole into the space between the mirrors. (If you didn't bother making a hole, just look over the top of one mirror.) You can also try placing either your finger or some other object between the mirrors.

If you place an object between the mirrors, notice that there is a repetitious pattern in the orientation and spacing of the images. Objects with contrasting colors on the front and back (such as red and white) show this well. Successive images alternate from front view to back view. If the original object is closer to one mirror than to the other, the distance between successive images will alternate from close together to far apart—making the images seem to be grouped in pairs, with a front side always facing a front side, or a back side always facing a back side.

What's Going On?

In this light-ray diagram, the solid lines show the actual path of the light rays; the dashed lines show the path of the light rays projected by your brain. You see images where the dashed lines come together.

This light-ray diagram shows the rays that come from the front of an object and those that come from the back. After the first reflection, you see one image in each mirror where the dashed lines come together (1). After the second reflection, you see a second image in each mirror (2), and so on.

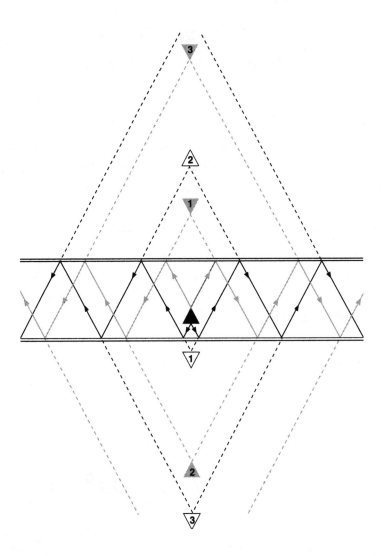

As you look at the images formed in one of the mirrors on the diagram, notice that there is an alternation of front and back views, that the images appear to be grouped in pairs, and that a front side is always facing a front side and a back side is always facing a back side. This corresponds to what you actually observe in the mirrors.

○ ○ ○ ○ ○ ○   **etc.**   ○ ○ ○ ○ ○ ○

An interesting variation on the version described involves gluing the two mirrors to a block of foam rubber. Mirrors 6 × 6 inches (15 × 15 cm) work well for this handheld portable version, but mirror size is not crucial. The foam should separate the mirrors by about 2 to 3 inches (5 to 8 cm).

An even simpler handheld version of this Snack uses pieces of sponge as spacers, with rubber bands holding the mirrors together. Use a soft sponge. The cheap ones used for washing cars work well. One or two holes can be drilled into the mirror.

Squeeze the foam so that the mirrors are not quite parallel to each other. You will see a pattern of images that curves off into infinity. Try it, you'll like it!

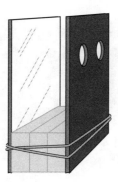

Magic Wand

See pictures in thin air.

▶ When you view a slide show or a movie, where is the picture? Is it on the film, in the air, on the screen, or in the eye of the viewer? This Snack will help you investigate and understand how you see.

Materials ▶ A slide projector.

▶ A 35 mm slide.

▶ A moveable screen. (A piece of white poster-board will do.)

▶ A pencil, wooden dowel, or meterstick.

Assembly
(15 minutes or less)

Place the moveable screen in the center of the room, about 6 feet (2 m) in front of the projector. Put the slide in the projector, turn the projector on, and focus the image on the screen. Then remove the screen.

This Snack works better if the light from the projector travels out through a door or window after it passes the point where the screen was.

To Do and Notice
(5 minutes or more)

Hold the wand horizontally in the place where the screen was located. Then wave the wand rapidly up and down by flicking your wrist. Notice that the picture appears as the wand moves.

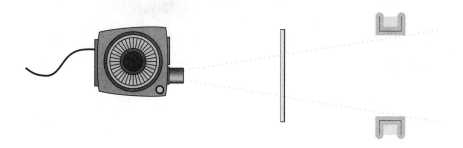

Wave the wand at an angle, or rotate it to trace out a cylinder or a cone. Notice the deformed image that you produce.

What's Going On?

The image is focused in the air. But you can't see the image unless something reflects the light to your eyes. The moving wand reflects the light just as the screen does, except that the wand reflects the image piece by piece.

When this reflected light enters your eyes, it makes an image on your retina. Your eyes retain each piece of the image for about $\frac{1}{30}$th of a second—long enough to let you put the pieces together to make a composite picture.

Your eyes' tendency to hang on to an image for a fraction of a second is called *persistence of vision*. Persistence of vision occurs because the light detectors in your eyes, the rods and the cones, continue to fire electrical signals to your brain even after a very short pulse of light has come and gone.

The deformed images produced when you move the rod in the shape of a cylinder or cone are examples of a map projection. The flat image of the slide is projected onto a curved surface. The resulting deformations are like those that occur when the spherical surface of the earth is mapped onto a flat map.

You might wonder if you could see the image by looking directly into the slide projector from the place where the screen used to be. The light in most projectors is too bright to try this experiment. However, the answer is no. Your eye can only make images of the light that actually enters the pupil. When you put your eyes where the screen was, only light from a small part of the image enters your eye. So you cannot see the entire image.

Persistence of vision is what allows you to see a
television picture. One bright dot of light, produced
when an electron beam collides with phosphors on
the inside front of the picture tube, sweeps across the
television screen. The dot sweeps across the screen
one horizontal line at a time, sweeping out the entire
525 lines that fill the picture area every $\frac{1}{30}$th of a
second. Yet you do not see a flying dot; you see
a complete picture.

   You can do a fun 3-D version of this Snack if the
slide you project is of a simple shape, such as a white
circle. Hold a stiff piece of white cardboard or foamcore board where the screen would be, and then
sweep the board back and forth through the image,
moving the flat side toward and away from the projector. The circle will become a white cylinder hanging
in space.

Parabolas

It's all done with mirrors.

▶ What you perceive as an object is really an image in space, created by two concave mirrors. This illusion would do credit to any magician.

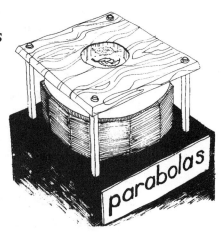

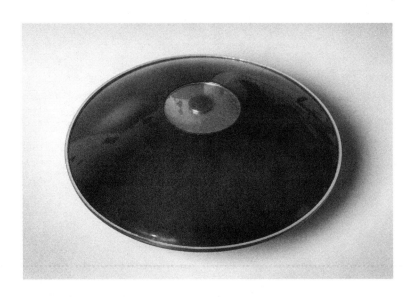

Materials ▸ Mirage Maker™ (available at the Exploratorium Store, or from Edmund Scientific as Optic Mirage™, or from the manufacturer: Opti-gone Associates, Inc., Woodland Hills, CA 91364; approximate price: $40).

Assembly

No assembly required.

Though the Mirage Maker™ unit is relatively expensive, this commercially available device is a great investment if you can afford it. Buying the unit is the only realistic way we could devise to replicate this exhibit. Large concave glass mirrors are available from scientific supply houses, but their cost approaches or exceeds that of the Mirage Maker™ device. (If you know of a reasonably priced source, please let us know!) But even if you did find a cheap source of glass mirrors, you would then have to cut a hole in the glass—a difficult task at best, and one that puts the mirror at risk.

To Do and Notice
(5 minutes or more)

Put an object in the bottom of the apparatus. A coin works well, but a small, colorful object that looks like a push-button, resting on a "PUSH" sign, is a creative alternative.

Notice that the object or button appears to be in the hole in the top of the device. Try to grab the object or push the button. There's nothing there!

What's Going On?

You are seeing an image formed by two concave mirrors facing one another. The object is placed at the center of the bottom mirror. The curvature of the mirrors is such that the object is at the focal point of the top mirror.

When light from a point on the object hits the top mirror, it reflects in parallel rays. These parallel rays hit the bottom mirror and reflect so that they reassemble to form a point located at one focal length from the bottom mirror. The mirrors are placed so that the focal point of the bottom mirror is located at the hole in the top of the device. The end result is that light from every point on the object is assembled into an image in the hole.

The ray diagram below may help explain this effect.

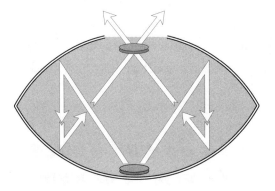

○ ○ ○ ○ ○ ○ ○ **etc.** ○ ○ ○ ○ ○ ○ ○

The image produced by this apparatus is known as a *real image*, because the light that forms it actually passes through the location of the image. However, if you place a piece of wax paper or onionskin paper at the location of the real image, the image will not appear on the paper. The outside regions of the mirrors that do not reflect light to your eyes do reflect light to the paper. The edges of the mirrors have large aberrations and create an image so blurred that it cannot be seen.

Pinhole Magnifier

Who needs expensive optical equipment?

► A pinhole in an index card can act like a magnifying glass, helping your eye focus on an object that is very close to you. However, by limiting the amount of light that reaches your eye from the object, the pinhole also makes the object appear dimmer.

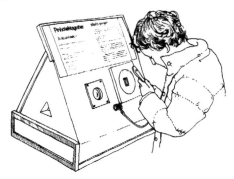

Materials
- ▶ A 3 × 5 inch (8 × 13 cm) file card.
- ▶ A straight pin or needle.
- ▶ Aluminum foil.
- ▶ A lamp with dim (10 to 25 watt) lightbulb.
- ▶ Masking tape.
- ▶ X-Acto™ knife, matte knife, or scissors.
- ▶ Adult help.

Assembly
(5 minutes or less)

Cut a hole about 1 inch (2.5 cm) square in a file card. Tape a piece of aluminum foil over the hole in the card and use the pin to punch a hole in the center of the foil. You can make a good pinhole by placing the foil on a thick piece of cardboard and rotating a needle.

To Do and Notice
(15 minutes or more)

Hold the card near your eye and look at the lightbulb several feet away. Move closer to the bulb until you almost touch it, and notice the magnified writing on the bulb. Use the pinhole magnifier to examine other small brightly lit objects. You can, for example, examine a computer screen or a television screen up close using a pinhole magnifier.

Try using pins or needles with different diameters to make different-sized holes. Notice that the smaller the pinhole is, the dimmer your view. As the pinhole is made smaller, the image at first becomes sharper, but then is blurred by diffraction.

You can even form a pinhole by curling your index finger. Or try this as a magnifier:

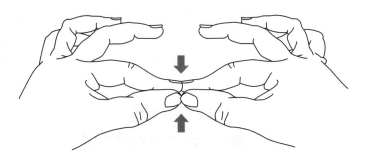

What's Going On?

The pinhole magnifier works on a very simple principle: The closer you get to an object, the bigger it looks to you. This is because the closer you are to the object, the larger the image the object forms on your retina (see Figure 1). Unfortunately, however, there is a limit to this. If you get too close to the object, your eye is not able to bend some of the light rays enough to obtain a focused image. As a result, the image becomes blurry or fuzzy (see Figure 2). The pinhole magnifier gets around this problem by limiting the rays that come to you from each part of the object (see Figure 3).

Sadly, there is a trade-off between the *resolution*, or sharpness, of the image and its brightness. A tiny pinhole produces a very sharp image, but because it cuts down on the number of rays that enter your eye, the pinhole makes the object look much dimmer.

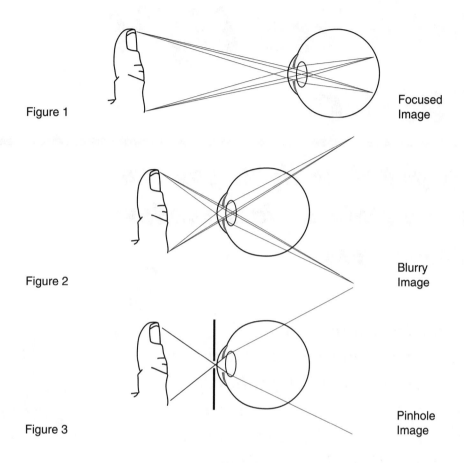

Figure 1

Focused
Image

Figure 2

Blurry
Image

Figure 3

Pinhole
Image

○ ○ ○ ○ ○ ○ **etc.** ○ ○ ○ ○ ○ ○

By using a pinhole magnifier, nearsighted people who
normally see things fuzzily at a distance will be able
to see them clearly; likewise, farsighted people who
normally see things fuzzily close up will be able to see
them clearly.

Polarized Light Mosaic

With polarized light, you can make a stained glass window without glass.

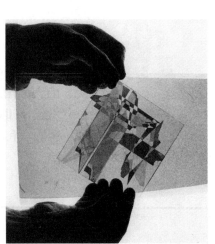

▶ Using transparent tape and polarizing material, you can make and project beautifully colored patterns reminiscent of abstract or geometric stained glass windows. Rotating the polarizer as you view the patterns causes the colors to change. With a little creativity, you can also create colorful renditions of objects or scenes.

Materials ▶ 2 sheets of polarizing material. (You can use two lenses from an old pair of polarizing sunglasses. However, since the lenses are small, the pattern or picture that you will be able to view will be limited in size. Larger polarizing filters are available from Edmund Scientific.)

▶ Transparent tape with a shiny, nonmatte surface. (Scotch™ brand tape will not work in this Snack. Some brands of inexpensive transparent tape—such as Le Page's Thrift-Tape™—will work. You will need to test the brand you choose. See the Assembly section for details.)

▶ A piece of glass or Plexiglas™. Plastic generally will not work. (See the Assembly section for details.)

▶ Overhead projector.

▶ Adult help.

Assembly
(15 minutes or less)

Before you buy large quantities of transparent tape, test the brand you are buying by placing a strip of the tape between two pieces of polarizing material. For convenience, you can actually stick the tape to one of the polarizers. Then rotate one of the polarizers against the other. If the tape changes from dark to light, or vice versa, when you rotate the polarizer, you can use the tape in this recipe. If the tape remains the same shade of darkness

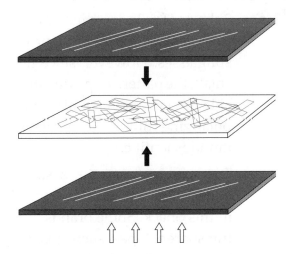

when you rotate the polarizer, the tape will not work in this Snack.

We make our patterns on glass or Plexiglas™ because these materials add no color to the design. Most plastic will not work as a backing material, since it produces colors in this situation. However, we have found that the transparent plastic tops of greeting card containers can be used successfully.

Put strips of tape on the piece of glass or Plexiglas™ in a crisscross or random pattern. Be sure that there are several areas where two or three strips of tape overlap and crisscross. Sandwich the glass between the polarizers; then place the resulting package on the overhead projector. Rotate the top polarizer and observe the color changes.

You can also use multiple layers of crisscrossed tape to create pictures. The tape can be cut as necessary so that it forms the desired shapes. You can also form letters and words.

What's Going On?

The colors that you see result from differences in the speed of polarized light as it travels through the transparent tape. In transparent tape, the long polymer molecules are stretched parallel to the length of the tape. Light polarized parallel to the stretch of the molecules travels through the tape more slowly than light polarized perpendicular to the stretch. (For an explanation of *polarization*, consult the *Polarized Sunglasses Snack*.)

Every material has an *index of refraction*—that is, the ratio of the speed of light in a vacuum to the speed of light in the material. Light travels through the tape you used in this demonstration at two different speeds. (Materials with this property are called *birefringent*, which is derived from the Greek words for "doubly refracting.")

When polarized light enters the tape, its direction of polarization will probably not line up with the length of tape. If the light is polarized in a direction that does not line up, its direction of polarization will be resolved into two perpendicular components. One of these components will be parallel to the length of the tape, and one will be perpendicular.

The waves that comprise these two components are initially in step with each other. But as they travel at different speeds through the tape, they become out of step. That is, the crest of one wave no longer lines up with the crest of the other. When these out-of-step light waves emerge from the tape on the other side, they recombine, making light with a different polarization than the original light's.

The thicker the tape is, the more out of step the components will become, and the greater the change in the polarization will be. If, for example, the two waves recombine after one has been delayed by one-half a wavelength, the direction of polarization of the light will be rotated by 90 degrees.

The white light shining from the overhead projector is made up of light of all different colors or wavelengths. Since the index of refraction of the tape is different for each color of light, each color has its own unique pair of speeds as it passes through the tape. The result is that the polarization of each color is changed by a different amount for a given thickness of tape.

When a second piece of polarizer is placed over the tape and rotated, it transmits different colors at different angles. This accounts for the color combinations that you see at a given angle, and for the changes in color as the polarizer is rotated.

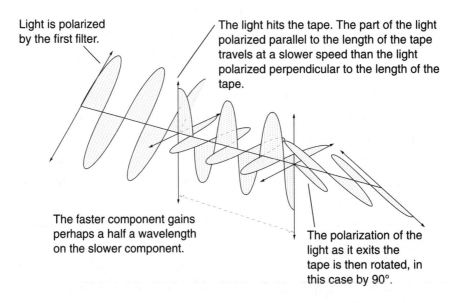

Light is polarized by the first filter.

The light hits the tape. The part of the light polarized parallel to the length of the tape travels at a slower speed than the light polarized perpendicular to the length of the tape.

The faster component gains perhaps a half a wavelength on the slower component.

The polarization of the light as it exits the tape is then rotated, in this case by 90°.

A wave diagram of polarized light passing through a birefringent tape.

The diagram on page 88 is similar to one found in Paul Hewitt's excellent book, *Conceptual Physics* (seventh edition, HarperCollins College Publishers, New York, 1993).

For more information, two excellent references are Hewitt's *Conceptual Physics,* and *Seeing the Light* by David Falk, Dieter Brill, and David Stork (Harper & Row, 1986, pp. 358–365).

You can adapt this technique for use with a 35 mm slide projector. Punch the film out of an old 35 mm slide and crisscross layers of tape over the opening. Place a piece of polarizing material inside the projector just in back of the slide and rotate a second piece in front of the lens. As the front polarizer is rotated, your creations will change colors. Colors are determined by the orientation of pieces and thickness of the layers. Rotate the polarizer to the rhythm of your favorite music, and you will have a creative, do-it-yourself light show.

Polarized Sunglasses

If you rotate a pair of polarizing sunglasses, you'll find that they cut road glare much better in some positions than in others.

▶ When light reflects from water, asphalt, or other nonmetallic surfaces, it becomes **polarized**. That is, the reflected light is usually vibrating more in one direction than in others. Polarizing sunglasses reduce this reflection, known as **glare**, but only when the polarizing lenses are oriented properly.

Materials ► 1 or 2 pieces of polarizing material (such as old lenses from polarizing sunglasses).

► 1 clear lightbulb with socket and cord.

► 1 piece of shiny, opaque plastic (the shiny black side of a cassette-tape case will work well).

Assembly

No assembly required.

To Do and Notice
(15 minutes or more)

Place the lit bulb with its filament parallel to the surface of the plastic. Orient the bulb so that you can see the reflection of the bulb in the plastic.

Look at the reflection through a piece of polarizer. Rotate the polarizer and vary the angle at which you look at the plastic until you get the dimmest reflection. You'll probably get the best results when there's about a 35-degree angle between your eyes and the piece of plastic (see the drawing on page 92). Rotate the polarizer 90 degrees as you watch the reflection. The reflection should become notably brighter.

Observe reflections elsewhere around you. Rotate the polarizer and vary the angle of viewing to vary the brightness. Try looking at a reflection from a metallic surface, such as an ordinary mirror. There should be no difference in the brightness of an image reflected in the mirror as you rotate the polarizer or vary the angle of viewing.

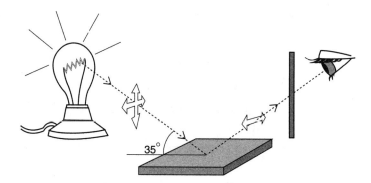

Look at the sky through the polarizing lens. Notice that the brightness of the sky changes as you rotate the polarizer. That's because the light in the sky is polarized. (For more information about this effect, see the *Blue Sky* Snack.)

Look through a polarizer at the surface of a pond on a bright, sunny day. Rotate the polarizer. Notice that at one orientation of the polarizer the surface reflections are greatly reduced and you can see beneath the surface of the water. Rotate the polarizer 90 degrees from this orientation, and the surface reflections block your view of the underwater world. This is why fishermen wear polarizing sunglasses.

What's Going On?

The lightbulb produces unpolarized light—each photon is vibrating in its own different direction. Nonmetallic surfaces, such as black plastic, tend to reflect light that is vibrating parallel to the surface and to transmit or absorb light vibrating in all other directions. If the black plastic is horizontal, then it reflects light that is vibrating horizontally, creating horizontally polarized light. The horizontal black plastic reflects less light that is vibrating vertically.

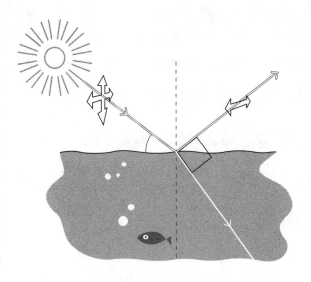

The polarizer lets through light that is vibrating in one direction and absorbs light that is vibrating in all other directions. When the black surface is horizontal, the reflection looks dimmest when you hold the filter so that it lets through just vertically vibrating light. The reflection looks brightest when you hold the filter so that it lets through just horizontally vibrating light.

Horizontal surfaces in the environment, such as the asphalt of a street or the surface of a lake, reflect light that is vibrating horizontally. Polarizing sunglasses absorb this horizontally oriented glare. If you tilt your head sideways, this horizontally oriented glare passes through the glasses, making the surface look brighter.

○ ○ ○ ○ ○ ○ **etc.** ○ ○ ○ ○ ○ ○

Light becomes completely polarized parallel to the surface at one particular angle of reflection, called *Brewster's angle*. Brewster's angle for water is 53 degrees; for glass it is 56 degrees; for plastic the angle varies but, in general, will be somewhere between these two angles. Brewster's angle is traditionally measured from a line that is perpendicular to the surface. To find the angle measured from the surface, you must subtract Brewster's angle from 90 degrees.

Rotating Light

Polarized light passing through sugar water "rotates" to reveal beautiful colors.

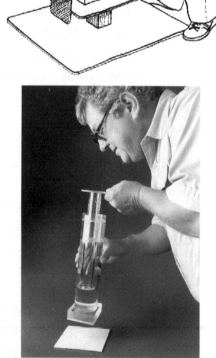

▶ White light is made up of all the colors in the rainbow. When polarized white light passes through a sugar solution, each color's direction of polarization is changed by a different amount. It is possible to see the colors change as the depth of the solution changes or as the polarizing filter is rotated.

Materials ▶ A clear plastic or glass (100 ml) graduated cylinder. (Or make your own using epoxy glue, plastic cement, or silicone seal, a square of clear plastic or glass about 3 × 3 inches [8 × 8 cm], and a 6 inch [15 cm] length of clear, rigid plastic tubing that is about 2 inches [5 cm] in diameter. See Assembly for instructions.)

▶ 2 pieces of polarizing material, such as the lenses from a pair of polarizing sunglasses.

▶ Karo® syrup.

▶ A light source. (Brightly illuminated sheet of white paper, overhead projector, or flashlight.)

▶ Optional: clear plastic cylinder 1 inch (2.5 cm) in diameter (either solid or hollow) with one closed end; colored filters; other liquids that can take the place of the Karo® syrup.

Assembly
(5 minutes or less if you use a graduated cylinder; 30 minutes or less if you make your own container)

If you are making your own container, attach one end of the plastic tube to the square of clear acrylic using epoxy, plastic cement, or silicone seal (see the diagram on page 96).

Fill the tube with several inches of Karo® syrup. Put one piece of polarizing material under the bottom of the base and hold the

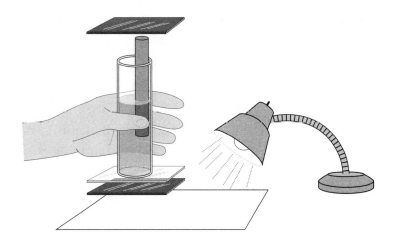

other above the top of the tube. Place a light source below the bottom polarizer.

To Do and Notice
(30 minutes or more)

Look down through the tube at the light source. Slowly rotate the polarizing filter and notice the color changes in the syrup.

Now hold the filter still and change the depth of the syrup. Pour more syrup into the tube. (If you have the optional tube or cylinder, you can push the cylinder or the closed end of the tube down into the solution.) Notice that the color changes with changes in the syrup's depth. If you rotate the filter and change the depth at just the right speeds, you should be able to keep the color constant.

You can perform a quantitative experiment by placing a colored filter under the tube. Suppose you use a blue filter. In order to see the blue as you add syrup, you must slowly rotate the upper polarizing filter. Determine the depth of syrup required to rotate the direction of polarization of blue light by one full turn.

Then try the same experiment with a red filter. With red light, a greater depth of syrup is needed.

Try a variety of transparent liquids and solutions such as honey and sugar syrup. Some are better than others at changing the direction of polarization.

What's Going On?

Light from most ordinary light sources wiggles up and down, left and right, and diagonally. Your polarizing filter lets through only the light that is vibrating in one particular direction. In this *polarized* light, the light waves all wiggle in the same direction.

To understand what this means, picture waves traveling along a rope. If the waves vibrate up and down, they are vertically polarized. Vertically polarized rope waves can pass through the slots between the vertical slats in a fence; waves vibrating in other directions are blocked by the slats. If you orient a polarizing filter properly, vertically polarized light waves can pass through the filter, while waves vibrating in other directions are blocked.

The light emerging from the light source at the bottom of the tube is unpolarized. That means that this light vibrates in all directions perpendicular to the light's direction of motion. The polarizing filter under the sugar solution polarizes this light, so that it vibrates in only one direction.

When polarized light passes through the Karo® syrup, the direction of its polarization is changed. Light vibrating from side to side, for example, might end up vibrating at a 45-degree angle. The amount of rotation depends on the depth of the syrup: the angle of rotation is proportional to the depth. It also depends on the concentration of the syrup: the more concentrated the syrup, the greater the rotation. Finally, the angle of rotation depends on the wavelength or color of the light. Blue light, with its shorter wavelength, rotates more than the longer-wavelength red light.

When the white light emerges from the sugar solution, each color in the light has its own direction of polarization. When viewed without a polarizing filter, this light still appears white, since our unaided eyes cannot detect the direction of polarization of light. However, when you look through a second polarizing filter, you see only the light that is vibrating in a direction that can pass through the filter. Only certain wavelengths or colors of light have the appropriate polarization. The intensity of the other colors in the light, which have different directions of vibration, is diminished. If a certain color of light has its polarization perpendicular to the axis of the polarizing filter, it is blocked out completely. (Think about the fence again. The rope waves won't get through if they are vibrating perpendicular to the slats.) As you rotate the filter, each orientation of the rotated filter produces a different dominant color, as does each different depth of sugar solution.

Materials that change the orientation of polarized light are called *optically active* materials. Some optically active solutions rotate the direction of polarization clockwise, to the right; others rotate it counterclockwise, to the left.

All organically produced glucose rotates the direction of polarization of light clockwise. This sugar is called *d-glucose*. Another sugar, called *l-glucose*, rotates the direction of polarization to the left. It can only be made by inorganic chemical synthesis. Both d-glucose and l-glucose have the same chemical formula: $C_6H_{12}O_6$. However, the atoms in each of these isomers are arranged in a different pattern. The left-handed sugar (l-glucose) tastes just as sweet as the right-handed one (d-glucose), but your body can't use it as an energy source. That's how left-handed sugars can produce sweetness without calories.

All of the proteins in your body and in all organisms on earth are made from amino acids that rotate the direction of polarization of light to the left. On the other hand, laboratory-synthesized amino acids, and amino acids found on meteorites, are made up of equal numbers of amino acids that rotate light to the right and amino acids that rotate light to the left. No one knows why this is so.

Soap Film Painting

A soap film becomes an ever-changing work of art.

▶ Under the influence of gravity, a thin film of soap constantly changes thickness, creating an ever-changing array of colors.

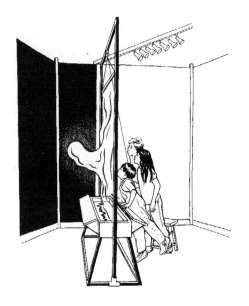

Materials
- One 24 inch (60 cm) length of 1 × 6 inch wood (common shelving) for base.
- Two 20 inch (50 cm) lengths of 1 × 2 inch wood for upright supports.
- One 24 inch (60 cm) length of 1 × 2 inch wood for overhead member.
- One 13 inch (32 cm) length of 1 × 2 inch wood for lower anchor.
- One 13 inch (32 cm) length of ⅜ inch (9 mm) diameter plastic pipe.
- One 15 inch (38 cm) plastic tray for bubble solution. (A Rubbermaid™ drawer insert works well.)
- 2 small screw eyes.
- Fishing line.
- Epoxy.
- Nails.
- Bubble solution made from ⅔ cup (150 ml) Dawn™ dishwashing liquid and 1 tablespoon glycerine (available in drugstores) in 1 gallon (3.8 liters) of water. (We have found that aging this solution for at least a day significantly increases the strength of the soap film.)
- Adult help.

Assembly
(1 hour or less)

Drill two small holes 11 inches (28 cm) apart in the 24 inch (60 cm) overhead member and the plastic pipe. Drill a single hole at

the center of the overhead
member. Drill a second set
of holes 1 inch (2.5 cm)
closer to the center of the
pipe. All the holes should
be large enough to let the
fishing line be inserted
through them, and to let the
line travel through them
freely when necessary.

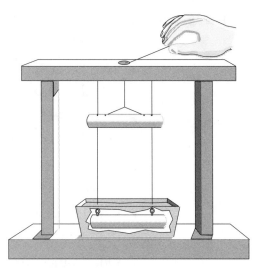

Epoxy the lower an-
chor into the plastic tray
and fix the screw eyes into
the wood 11 inches (28 cm) apart.

Assemble the base and upright supports and nail the overhead member into position (see the diagram above and the
photo on page 100).

Tie lengths of fishing line to the screw eyes. Thread the pipe
on, then thread the line through the outside holes in the overhead member and knot them in place. Make the lines as taut as
possible to allow the pipe to travel freely up and down.

Run another piece of fishing line down through one of the inside holes in the pipe and up through the other hole. Tie a slip
knot to form a noose. Run the free end of the line up through the
hole in the center of the overhead member to act as a lifting cord
(see diagram).

Fill the plastic tray with bubble solution until at least the entire lower half of the pipe is submerged.

To Do and Notice
(15 minutes or more)

Pull the string and raise the bar out of the soapy water to make
a soap film.

Notice the changing colors reflected by the film. The colored patterns in the vertical soap film are most easily seen by standing with your back to a white surface and viewing the soap film against a black background.

Shake the frame back and forth repeatedly. Notice the pattern of waves on the film.

Stand a few feet away from the film and blow on it gently. The film stretches out into a bulge when you blow and returns to its original flat shape when you stop.

What's Going On?

A soap film is a soapy water sandwich, with two outside layers of soap molecules forming boundaries around a layer of soapy water. The thickness of the soap film changes as the water drains down the inside of the film. When light strikes the front surface of the bubble film, some of the light is reflected (about 4%). The remainder of the wave is transmitted through to the rear surface. At the rear surface of the soap film, more of the light is reflected back to your eyes. The light reflecting from the front of the film meets up with the light reflecting from the back of the film, and the waves combine.

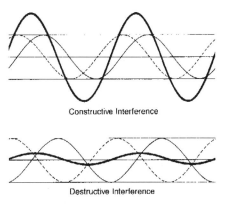

Constructive Interference

Destructive Interference

The beautiful colors you see on the soap film are due to *interference patterns*, created when light reflects off the two surfaces of the thin soap film. Interference patterns are created when two reflected waves line up *in phase* or *out of phase*.

If two waves line up in phase, with crests together and troughs together, we say that the waves are *interfering constructively.* When two waves line up out of phase, crest to trough, we say that the waves are *interfering destructively.*

White light can be considered a mixture of three additive primary colors: red, green and blue. If the thickness of the soap film is just right to cause the destructive interference of one of the additive primaries, you will perceive a mixture of the two remaining colors:

$$\text{white} - \text{red} = \text{blue} + \text{green} = \textit{cyan} \text{ (bluish green)}$$
$$\text{white} - \text{green} = \text{red} + \text{blue} = \textit{magenta} \text{ (reddish blue)}$$
$$\text{white} - \text{blue} = \text{red} + \text{green} = \textit{yellow}$$

Therefore, everywhere you see yellow, the film is just the right thickness to destructively remove the blue light waves. Where you see cyan, the red light has been destructively removed. And where you see magenta, the green light has been destructively removed.

Spectra

Fingerprints for light sources.

▶ *Using a diffraction grating, you can observe that what seems to be a single color of light may really be a combination of colors, called a* **spectrum**. *You can also compare the spectra produced by different light sources.*

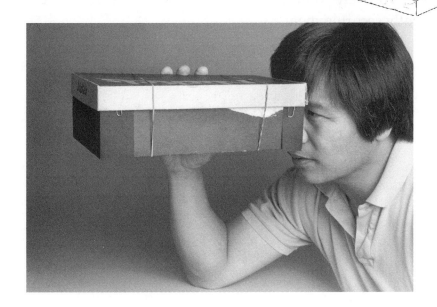

Materials ► A shoe box or a mailing tube about 2 inches (5 cm) in diameter and about 1 foot (30 cm) long.

► Diffraction grating (you can obtain this in sheet form or slide-mounted from Edmund Scientific or the Exploratorium Store).

► Index cards.

► Tape.

► Scissors or matte knife.

► Adult help.

Assembly
(30 minutes or less)

At one end of the shoe box or mailing tube, cut a rectangular hole measuring about ¾ inch (2 cm) wide by 1½ inches (3.5 cm) high. Cover the hole with pieces of index card to create a vertical slit about ³⁄₁₆ inch (5 mm) wide. Tape these pieces lightly in place for now, since you may want to adjust the width of the slit before permanently securing them.

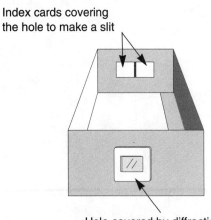

Index cards covering
the hole to make a slit

Hole covered by diffraction grating

At the opposite end from the slit, cut an opening measuring about 2 × 2 inches (5 × 5 cm). Cover this opening with a piece of grating material cut from a sheet, or with a slide-mounted grating. It is important that the scratches on the grating are parallel to the slit in the other end of the tube or box, but you may not be able to judge this until you try out your device. Tape the grating lightly in place for now, and move it if necessary as directed below.

If you are using a shoe box, put the top on the box. Hold the shoe box or the tube so that the slit is facing a light source. An ordinary incandescent lamp is a good starter. Be sure the slit is oriented vertically.

Look through the diffraction grating into the box or the tube. You should see colors. The spectrum of the light source should extend to the left and right of the slit. If you don't see the spectrum extending to both sides, the scratches on the grating are not parallel to the slit. Turn the grating one-quarter turn and look again. Adjust further as necessary until the spectrum extends to the left and right of the vertical slit, and then tape the grating securely in place.

Adjust the slit width until you obtain a spectrum that is both reasonably bright and reasonably well defined.

The final device is a simple *spectroscope*, a device used for forming and examining the unique combination of colors that make up any light. These colors are called a *spectrum* (plural: *spectra*).

To Do and Notice
(30 minutes or more)

Compare the spectra of various sources. When you view different light sources, look for specific colors and notice the spacing between colored lines. The heated tungsten filament of an incandescent lightbulb produces a continuous spectrum, and one color shades into another. The electrically excited mercury vapor in a fluorescent bulb produces distinct colored lines; the phosphors that coat the inside of the bulb produce a continuous spectrum.

Some other suggested light sources are a candle flame, the flame from a Bunsen burner, a flashlight, a camping lantern, yellow streetlights (sodium produces the color), blue streetlights (mercury vapor produces the color), neon signs, and slide projector lamps.

Different light sources produce different spectra. You can see the solar spectrum by looking at sunlight reflecting off a piece of white paper. DO NOT LOOK DIRECTLY AT THE SUN!

What's Going On?

When atoms of different materials are excited by electric current or other sources of energy, they glow with a unique spectrum. Atoms of different elements have different colors in their spectra. These characteristic color patterns represent specific atoms just as fingerprints serve to identify different people.

A diffraction grating acts like a prism, spreading light into its component colors. The light that you see from a light source is the sum of all these colors. Each color corresponds to a different frequency of light. The diffraction grating sorts light by frequency, with violet light (the highest frequency of visible light) at one end of the spectrum and red light (the lowest frequency of visible light) at the other.

When atoms in a dilute gas (like the mercury vapor in a mercury street light) radiate light, the light can be seen through a diffraction grating as a *line spectrum*, made up of bright lines of color. Each line in the spectrum of such a gas corresponds to one frequency of light emission, and is produced by an electron changing energy levels in the atom.

In solids, liquids, and densely packed gases, the situation is not so simple. As an atom emits light, it collides with other atoms. This changes the frequency of the light it emits. That's why solids, liquids, and dense gases have broad bands of light in their spectra.

○ ○ ○ ○ ○ ○   **etc.**   ○ ○ ○ ○ ○ ○

In addition to examining commonly available light sources, you might want to examine the spectra produced by specific gases. Power supplies and a variety of gas tubes are sold by scientific supply companies. The 1994 prices from the Frey Scientific Catalog are $136 for a power supply and about $20 for a gas tube. (To contact Frey Scientific, call 1-800-225-FREY.)

As an inexpensive alternative to sheet or slide-mounted diffraction grating, you might try Rainbow Glasses, sold at the Exploratorium Store for about $1.25.

Spherical Reflections

Discover art and science in a myriad of spherical reflections.

▶ Silver Christmas tree balls packed together in a single layer in a box create an array of spherical reflectors. Each sphere reflects a unique image of the world. Study the properties of spherical mirrors while you create a colorful mosaic of reflections.

Materials ► Silver Christmas tree balls (hooks and collars removed).

► A box with sides higher than the diameter of the balls.

► A sheet of styrofoam (cooked oatmeal which has been cooled can be used as a more ecological substitute).

► Black construction paper or flat black paint. (Be sure to use latex paint if the paint is to be used on the styrofoam. Oil-based paint will dissolve the styrofoam.)

Assembly
(30 minutes or less)

Cut the styrofoam to fit the bottom of the box. (If you prefer not to use styrofoam, pour in freshly cooked oatmeal thick enough to embed the neck of each bulb—about ½ inch (1 cm) thick—and let it cool.) Cover the styrofoam or oatmeal with a piece of black construction paper cut to size, or paint the styrofoam or oatmeal flat black. Lay the balls in the box in a single layer, packed as closely as possible. Gently but firmly push the stem end of each ball into the styrofoam or oatmeal so that the stem is held securely. (If you're using construction paper, push the stem end of each ball into the construction paper so that it makes a mark, and then cut the paper at the marked points to make insertion into the foam easier.)

To Do and Notice
(5 minutes or more)

Look at the spherical mirrors from various angles. Notice that the image in each mirror is a little different from the image in the neighboring mirrors. That's because each mirror "sees" the world from a slightly different vantage point. Notice that if you point your finger at one sphere, the image of your finger in all the other mirrors will point at the chosen mirror.

Also notice that your image is very small in the mirrors, and that it appears quite far away.

What's Going On?

Each Christmas tree ball is a convex mirror—a mirror that curves out toward the source of light. Convex mirrors reflect images that are smaller than life-sized.

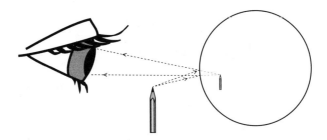

In the ray diagram above, notice the reflection of two rays of light from a particular point at the tip of the pencil. Your eye and brain follow these reflected rays backward along a straight line to their apparent intersection behind the mirror. All other reflected rays from the point also seem to originate at this intersection. The reflected rays from all other points on the pencil also appear to intersect at specific points behind the mirror. All these intersection points put together create what's called a *virtual image.*

Convex rearview car mirrors have a written warning cautioning that objects are actually closer than they appear. Your brain assumes that when an object that is known to be large—a car, for instance—has a small image in a mirror then the object is far away. In a convex mirror, however, an image that appears quite small can actually be very close.

Convex mirrors are often used as security mirrors in stores, since they reveal a broad field of view.

Touch the Spring

You can see the spring, but you can't touch it!

▶ *In the Exploratorium's* Touch the Spring *exhibit, a spring is placed in front of a concave mirror. The actual spring is not visible to the viewer, but the viewer can see the mirror image of the spring formed in space. When you try to touch the spring, you are attempting to touch an image. Your hand moves right through what seems to be a solid object! This is a magician's illusion at its finest. Here, we substitute a lightbulb for the spring.*

Touch the Spring

Materials ▶ A 16 inch (40 cm) diameter concave mirror (available from scientific supply houses for about $40).

▶ Wood to build a support stand for the mirror and a small box for the lightbulb. (See photo and drawings.)

▶ 2 light sockets, one with an electrical cord and plug.

▶ A lightbulb, 40 to 75 watts.

▶ One 3 × 5 inch (8 × 13 cm) card.

▶ Adult help.

Assembly
(1 hour or less)

Make a small wooden box with one open side as shown in the drawing. The height of the box should be slightly less than half the height of the mirror, and it should be wide enough and deep enough to hold the light bulb. Paint all surfaces of the box black.

Mount the socket that has no electrical cord or plug so that it

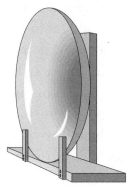

is centered on top of the box. Mount the other socket (the one with the cord and plug) upside-down inside the box, directly beneath the empty socket, as shown in the drawing.

Build the mirror support as shown in the drawing, and place the mirror in it.

To Do and Notice
(30 minutes or more)

Plug in the lightbulb and place the box with its open side facing the mirror. To find the focal length of the mirror, place the mirror far from the lightbulb—at least 20 feet (6 m)—so that its concave (hollow) side is facing the lightbulb. The mirror will then make a real image of the lightbulb close to the focal point of the mirror. Find the distance from the center of the mirror to the image of the lightbulb, and you will find the focal length of the mirror.

To find the location of the image, take a 3 × 5 inch (8 × 13 cm) card and hold it near the center of—and touching—the surface of the mirror. Move the card slowly away from the mirror. When the image of the bulb is in sharp focus, the card is near the focal point.

Place the mirror two focal lengths from the lightbulb. The concave mirror will reflect an image of the glowing bulb. This image will appear in space in front of the mirror. By carefully adjusting the vertical and horizontal position of the box, you can position the image so that it appears to be in the empty socket on top of the box. (You may have to place magazines or books under the box to adjust its height.)

The illusion works best in a darkened room. Have people stand back about 15 feet (5 m) so that they see a bulb in the upper socket. Then have them move slowly toward the bulb. They may have to bend or straighten slightly or move right or left slightly to maintain an undistorted image. When they are about 6 feet (2 m) from the image of the bulb, pass your hand through it. The illusion of your hand passing right through a lightbulb is impressive, even when everything is out in the open.

In the Exploratorium exhibit, everything is inside a large cabinet. To touch the image, you must reach through a small opening. The cabinet hides all the clues and enhances the illusion, but is a more elaborate construction project with associated storage problems.

What's Going On?

The image you see is formed by the concave spherical mirror. Light rays spreading out from one point on the lightbulb are reflected by the concave mirror so that they come back together at a point in space—creating a *real image* of that point.

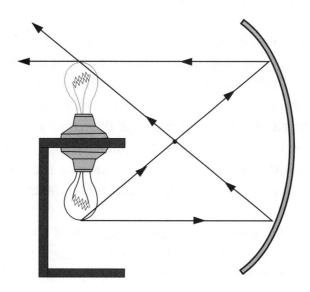

The rays continue on through this convergence point and strike your eye. The lens of your eye brings the rays together once again to create an image on your retina. Your eye and brain can't tell the difference between a retinal image of the reflected bulb and a retinal image of the actual bulb.

In some respects, however, the reflected image of the light-bulb differs from the actual bulb. Placing an object behind the reflected image will obscure the lightbulb. Many people feel queasy when they see this seemingly unnatural occurrence.

Though we use a lightbulb here, you can also make a real image of a nonglowing object. A small plastic animal, like a toy cow or pig, can be fun to use. You can add an additional flourish by shining a flashlight onto the image of the toy animal. A spot of light will appear on the image! The mirror collects the light from the flashlight and then images it onto the real toy animal.

A closely related Exploratorium exhibit that you can create with the same concave mirror is called *Shake Hands with Yourself.* In this exhibit, your hand is placed two focal lengths from a concave mirror, resulting in a real, inverted image the same size as your hand. This image is also located two focal lengths from the mirror. Thus, your actual hand can touch the image of your hand, and you can "shake hands with yourself."

In 1990 Nakamura began selling a small plastic par-abolic mirror with which to make miniature versions of the *Touch the Spring* exhibit. Related Snack: *Parabolas.*

Water Sphere Lens

Make a lens and a magnifying glass by filling a bowl with water.

▶ In the 1700s, spherical glass bottles filled with water were used to focus candlelight for fine work such as lace making. Round bottles of water, left in an open window, have been known to start fires by focusing sunlight into an intense "hot spot."

Materials ▸ A Florence (round-bottomed) flask or transparent spherical bowl, such as a fishbowl.

▸ A candle or a clear lightbulb with socket.

▸ A white card to use as a viewing screen.

▸ Water.

▸ A sheet of newspaper.

▸ Adult help.

Assembly
(1 minute or less)

Fill the flask or fishbowl with water to make a water sphere lens.

To Do and Notice
(15 minutes or more)

Place the light source (the lightbulb or the candle) more than 1 foot (30 cm) from the water sphere lens. Hold the white card against the side of the lens opposite the light source. Move the card away from the sphere until you see an image of the filament (or flame) on the card. Notice that the image is inverted.

Move the light source up and notice that its image moves down.

Move the light very close to the water sphere, and notice that you cannot find an image on the card at any distance.

Look through the water sphere lens at a newspaper held close to the other side of the sphere. Notice that the sphere acts as a magnifying glass. Vary the light-to-lens distance and notice how the image-to-lens distance changes. Also notice how the image changes size.

What's Going On?

Light rays from the bulb or candle bend when they enter the water-filled sphere, and bend again when they leave the sphere, as shown in the diagram below. The only light rays that don't bend are the ones that enter the sphere at a straight-on, 90-degree angle—that is, the ones that pass through the center of the bowl.

The sphere acts just like a lens, focusing the light that passes through into an image on the other side. The image must lie on a straight line from the object through the center of the lens.

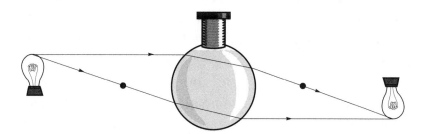

The image is upside down and reversed right to left. The motion of the image is also reversed: When the object moves up, the image moves down; when the object moves closer to the sphere, the image moves farther away. It might help to picture a seesaw: When one side moves up, the other side moves down.

Every lens has a *focal point,* which is a spot where light rays from far away converge after passing through the lens. The distance from the center of the lens to the focal point is called the *focal length.* Measure the focal length of your lens by finding a bright light source that's more than 30 feet (9 m) away. Using the white card, find the distance from the lens to the image. This is

the focal length. If you use the sun as your light source, the focused sunlight may be hot enough to burn the paper card. Be careful!

If an object is closer than one focal length to the center of the water sphere lens, the lens can't bend the light rays from the object enough to bring them back together to form an image. However, when you look through the water sphere lens at a nearby object, the lens of your eye can complete the bending, forming an image on your retina. The image on your retina made with the help of the water sphere lens is larger than the largest image you could make with your eye alone. The water sphere lens is thus a magnifying glass.

○ ○ ○ ○ ○ ○ **etc.** ○ ○ ○ ○ ○ ○

The image you see may be fuzzy and distorted, but should be recognizable. It also may show color distortion. The fuzziness is due to *spherical aberration,* and the colors are due to *chromatic aberration.*

Index

Page numbers in italics indicate illustrations relevant to the topic.